The Jesus-Healer

(1919)

James Leith Macbeth Bain

ISBN 0-7661-0586-5

Request our FREE CATALOG of over 1,000
Rare Esoteric Books
Unavailable Elsewhere

Freemasonry * Akashic * Alchemy * Alternative Health * Ancient Civilizations * Anthroposophy * Astral * Astrology * Astronomy * Aura * Bacon, Francis * Bible Study * Blavatsky * Boehme * Cabalah * Cartomancy * Chakras * Clairvoyance * Comparative Religions * Divination * Druids * Eastern Thought * Egyptology * Esoterism * Essenes * Etheric * Extrasensory Perception * Gnosis * Gnosticism * Golden Dawn * Great White Brotherhood * Hermetics * Kabalah * Karma * Knights Templar * Kundalini * Magic * Meditation * Mediumship * Mesmerism * Metaphysics * Mithraism * Mystery Schools * Mysticism * Mythology * Numerology * Occultism * Palmistry * Pantheism * Paracelsus * Parapsychology * Philosophy * Plotinus * Prosperity & Success * Psychokinesis * Psychology * Pyramids * Qabalah * Reincarnation * Rosicrucian * Sacred Geometry * Secret Rituals * Secret Societies * Spiritism * Symbolism * Tarot * Telepathy * Theosophy * Transcendentalism * Upanishads * Vedanta * Wisdom * Yoga * *Plus Much More!*

KESSINGER PUBLISHING, LLC

http://www.kessingerpub.com

email: books@kessingerpub.com

I AM ALPHA.

Spirit-communion is a reality of being, that can be, and should be so tested and proved as to satisfy all the demands of the most sane and keen judgment.

"It is needful that I go from you; for if I go not away I cannot return unto you in the fulness of my new power."—*Jesus Christ to his lovers.*

This portrait of the pure and gentle companion of our work of healing when in her virgin power we can now give, for this white soul of child-like beauty and most dainty modesty was born into the higher life on 4th September 1918, and the song of the welcome of her own angel-comrades in healing to the sweeter air and holier sun of their more blessed country has so sung its joy even in our human nature that no tear of sorrow has bedimmed our vision of her blessedness. And indeed to tell true, the angel-soul of this good woman is with me now more intimately, effectively and abidingly in my work than ever heretofore, and this is no more than the fulfilling of her promise to me. As will be seen, this portrait is an enlargement from a small one; yet, not-withstanding the imperfections incident to an enlargement, we find it to be the best likeness we have of the earth-form of Christ's Lily of the Healing Hand.

P.S.—I insert this portrait in a limited number of this book for it is only for the eye of the lover. And I ask the friend into whose hand this portrait comes to keep it, even for love's sake, from the gaze of the merely curious.

THE JESUS-HEALER
THE INBORN OF OUR NATURE

Being a mosaic of simple and spontaneous
thoughts, supplementary and complementary
to the teaching contained in
"The Brotherhood of Healers" and in
"The Christ of the Healing Hand,"
that have come to me these days and that
I give to you even as they came in their
own live words to me concerning
the work of the holy Jesus-light
as the power of the one and only
Healer of man in the Christ of
his whole nature.

---

*Before we can be acceptable as servants of love, we must, with the
full consent of our understanding and our will, have put our
old selfhood with all his prides and inane belongings
under the feet of the lowliest soul, for*

"Jesus from the ground suspires,"

*and the Jesus in us is always lowlier than the
lowliest of our kind.*

JAMES LEITH MACBETH BAIN.

London:
THE THEOSOPHICAL PUBLISHING HOUSE,
1 Upper Woburn Place, W.C. 1.

1919.

The oblation of our good.

To all the lovers and healers of man and beast, to all who, because of their love of the whole creation, are ordained of the one Christ-Spirit to this most holy service of Life, I offer the use of this continuation of our walk and our talk together in the Garden of the Healing Spirit.

There is no copyright on any of my writings, for they belong to every soul who needs them and who can use them for its blessing. Only unto this end have they been given me.

Therefore no one who uses them in any way for the service of the neighbour need ask my permission for so doing. And anyone can use them in translation or reproduce them in any way without even naming me.

Now I mean just what I say here. And I am greatly gladdened to find that in this I am taken at my word by comrades beyond the seas, who have translated my writings into their tongue, and that without even troubling me to give my consent. This is just as I would have it be, and these comrades do understand me. For I know that in the exercise of this communal principle no one could be found so base as to use these writings for any personal gain.

For they are no more mine than they are thine, human soul, dear to thy Christ, in whose name and in whose Will of Blessing they are now sent forth even for the service of thy need.

* * *

Since printing the above "The Lady Sheila" has been brought out in Braille by the National Society for the Blind, but I think that their readers would be better served by a print of "The Brotherhood of Healers," and this is being done.

* * *

While I recognise the gentle consideration of the great majority of the readers of my books in not writing me unnecessary letters, I would invite anyone who desires much to write me to do so without fail, for verily I would be the servant of every soul.

Ere the Cock Crow twice.

Truly a new day, a new order has come to our world, for the Dissolver has already dissolved the past form, and the Builder of the new is working, and we know it in all places of our present existence.

We know well it is so; and yet the day breaks and the sun arises, and the master chanticleer awakens as of old the sleeping children of nature at the very hour in which Jesus looked into the eye of Peter.

And again the gentle Lover looks into our eye, but this time we can say: O gentle Lover, thou hast won our whole nature, and henceforth we are the servants of thy will. For now that thy strength is our strength and our will thy will, we are able to stand in the hour of trial.

✠ ✠ ✠

And the lark sings his song far up there, hid in the darksome clouds of early dawn, and far away in the deep forest skraykes forth the wild soul of the pheasant, and the cuckoo brings even to our beds the note of the south, so that the great symphony of our woodlands hymn of praise may be whole.

And the Ancient of the great ocean utters too, as in the ages of the past, his mighty word of the eternities, hushing for the stillness of the night all other voices in his lullaby of peace.

only testimony I never weary of fulfilling even in these days of travail, what has touched me most during these years is the love I receive through the human soul. Often the sense of this is almost too much for me to bear, for I feel it is the sweetness of the Christ-child in these brothers and sisters that is giving me of its very best, pouring forth its choicest to this same Christ in me; and the cry of this human soul cannot but so often be :—I am not worthy of it all.

Especially during these days of our great personal and universal agony, this one holy Thing of God has made itself more intensely and more vividly real to me than heretofore; and the beauty of this flower of the human garden has been brought home so very intimately to this soul that I cannot but tell you of it. Surely, surely, this is the Spirit of the same Jesus-lover both as child and as mother in these gentle vessels, giving me of its very best, making to me, so very modestly as hardly to be guessed to be there, a gift of its sweetest fragrance. And surely it is the same lover in this man, coming to finer and fuller power of perception, that enables me to feel, realise, and assimilate this holy substance, this live food of God for the deathless Child of the soul.

Lovers, yes many lovers here; but these chaste vessels are God-lovers, and sure as it is a God-love it can kindle no jealousy, it can feed no flame of hate in any one.

Ah, but it is a great and a beautiful wonder, even the mystery of holy Love, and we are comforted to know that we can never fathom the deep of God.

So beautiful, so beautiful, O child of the ages, is this holy Thing that hath come to me even through your humanity, that no words of mine can tell how beautiful it is to your brother and lover in God.

☖ ☖ ☖

Now, to resume our theme, I declare to you, my friend and lover, whoever you be, that there is no personal relationship so near or so real to my inner nature as is this most intimate one of the soul-friend or Jesus-lover.

And that in this degree of my human unfoldment it is verily a personal relationship, and that in some hidden way this man here is actually in live, personal contact with the one known in history as Jesus of Nazareth, I am as far from denying as from asserting, for in these inner degrees of the mystery of our psychè the universal includes and covers the personal, and the cosmic never eliminates but always involves its microcosmic correspondencies.

Yes friend, I know I have found the Jesus-lover, the deathless, ageless, Love-light whom no critcism can take from me, as in my youth that of the divinity halls certainly did, and without doubt served me well in so doing.

And I know not a few who in these days have come even as I to the consciousness of the personal presence of this continuous and never passing Jesus-love-light apart from any necessary connection with any historical personality, and who indeed know Christ no longer after the flesh—such knowledge being to them in no way vital, but as one born within their own human nature, and thus inalienably theirs, ay, their very own, even the soul of their soul, the mind of their mind, the heart of their heart, the will of their will, the health of their whole being. For, as it is said: "It is needful for you that I go in order that I may come to you in all the unlimited power of Spirit."

Thus, friends and lovers dear in God, have I spoken in these pages as plainly as words may, and I leave it there, well satisfied with the sure fact of an unfailing experience which gives the constant, abiding fellowship of one who is closer to me than any human soul ever can be.

✢ ✢ ✢

Now I know that even in thus writing to you of my innermost love I am giving in very fact my best to you, and thus in the degree of our old selfhood parting with it. For, as every artist knows, once the darling beauty of the soul, be it in a melody, a picture, a poem, or in any other form, has been made a gift to all, it ceases to be to your own personal soul the intimate, secret delight that it was while as your nursling you cherished it there; so I know that in a manner I must in my personal soul feel the loss of this most secret intimacy, and might even be tempted to cry out: "I have given my strength and my beauty away."

But is not the whole mystery of the one great, true, and only Life-mode possible to us hid just in this very strange word?

For is it not in this very lavishing on the other of one's own innermost and best, in this sacrificing of the darling of our heart to the need of whomsover hath need that the larger, the truer, ay, the only way of the blessed life is? Indeed, indeed, the artist thus gives away his very soul, yet he who would keep the beauty or strength of his soul for himself shall lose it, and he who lavishes it on whomsoever can receive it keeps it forever as an inalienable good in the realm that passeth never away; and this is the realm of what we name the selfless Love.

☩ ☩ ☩

And now human soul, whosover you be, I wish to say to you as plainly as words can, for though I have said it often and plainly heretofore, I find it is still necessary to speak it, I am your brother, and as human a brother in every sense of the word as ever walked on this earth, experiencing just as you, the manifold infirmities and limitations of our incarnation.

And let all who love me note well that no greater pain can you inflict on my soul than to esteem me in any sense of the word other than your own human brother.

There are those who seem to love worship, but I tell you, in the name of the One who is Truth, it is most loathsome to me.

And the more I have tasted of this holy indwelling Presence the more has this sweet and sane and truly beautiful sense of our common humanity possessed my will and my love.

And, sure as the unspoken yet ever uttered prayer of our nature is that we be kept in this sweet and sane and holy beauty of humility we may be sure that we shall be kept in that place of true power, even the power to heal and give the whole goodness of God.

Well, well do I know that all of this man has not yet come into the wholeness of the Christ-beauty; well, well do I know that my elements are not yet all regenerate; well, well do I know that these hosts of powers in my nature have not yet all become subject to the will of the holy Christ of my nature. Nor is this in any way a source of despair, for I also know as well, ay, as well, that my Lover is my Redeemer, that my own Friend is my Healer.

✠ ✠ ✠

Many, many are the beautiful souls whom the Great Love has allowed me to meet in this day's journey through Life, and my one feeling for the high privilege of their fellowship is that of gratitude to the good hand. Specially what I owe to the sweet, clean fellowship of those gentle souls who have, for very love of the creature more than for love of self, long since eschewed all flesh foods, I can never, never tell.

For I know that in the holy cause which they represent, Christ my Healer has worked in and through their beauty for the cleansing of my nature from the power of many low desires and tendencies as well as from the actual love of flesh as a food, and I know that in their whole nature and through manifold experiences of pain and of privation in these superfine natures many of them are suffering though little they ween it is so, intensely and long, for and because of sins not their own, thus fulfilling in their very flesh the great service of the Lover and Healer of man.

For the greatest good that we can desire for ourself or for any other is that we become the true servant of every soul whosoever, wheresoever, or howsoever that soul may be, that we ever be found ready or at least willing to do our best there.

And this is the high distinction that we now seek for our own motherland, even as for all who by nature are nearest to our heart, ay, and for all these peoples, as for every soul we love in God, even this, that they be found worthy to be the servants of Love to all who have need.

✠ ✠ ✠

And now I would speak to you just a few words here, because there is need, concerning this the most high distinction to which you and I can come in the present degree of our nature's unfoldment, even this will and power to serve in Love all who need the service, and which we name the Christ-ministry. For the children need never have any difficulty in knowing those who are ordained of Christ, the One and only Ordainer, to be shepherds or servants of their spiritual need; for there is one sure sign, unmistakeable, unfailing, never-wanting of this ordination, and it is the pure, simple, child-like humility of the Lord of Love, wherein that last of all the old dwellers in man-soul to be cast out, even spiritual pride, is utterly eliminated from these human vessels.

To these servants of Love this grace of the beauty of a perfect health or sanity is as unassumed, as free, as true as the air they breathe; it is as natural to them as the flesh they wear.

No pretensions here nor assumptions of powers occult, mysterious; no pompous standing apart, and patronisingly allowing the little brother to approach thy more holy presence.

Nay, nay, the old worship of the creature, wherein we have seen, even in the streets of London, one man kneel before another, has passed and gone for ever. It is the lie that has no more place in the children of the new Day. For the word once spoken yet remains the one word:—" Let him who is the greater or elder among you be the servant," or as in the word of the holy Krishna-genius:—" Let him be lowlier than the grass." For I the Lord of Life am the servant of Life, and I the Master of Love am the servant of Love in thee.

Nothing could be farther away from the truth than to represent the masters as in any way unapproachable.

They are indeed our very brothers, and it is with them even as it is with you and with me, the farther on we go in the way of Life, the simpler, more childlike, more approachable by all, yes by all, we become. For I trow, these little children were as much at home with the blessed Jesus as they were with one another.

✠ ✠ ✠

For verily in these days of the one great and holy fellowship in Christ the Worker, even the fellowship of labour, we are in the very passing of the hoary power of priestcraft, and are witnesses of the dissolving of all that in the spirit of a pretentious superiority would set itself apart from sharing in the common services of life. This we have at least learned from these very simplicities of life and the health for body and mind that we have found therein, and of a truth, found only therein.

No longer shall man or woman be held in subjection to any pretention to the exclusive wearing of the robe of sanctity in the fulfilling of the priestly office to his fellows.

Nay, verily, for he who would be priest of God to his brethren in life must now follow the rule of the Jesus-lover, working with his own hands even as these his fellows work for their daily bread, and even as we are told the apostles of the Jesus-regime worked.

And just because I am your qualified and professed

teacher or guide in spiritual things I can in no way differentiate between thee and me in work or in food, in garb or in social status.

Now this is far-reaching as a power for the liberation of service, and it all comes from the understanding of the truth of the one fellowship of labour in Christ. What this unbinding of the human soul from the bonds of the priest means for the liberation of the powers of our womanhood for the service she alone can render is more than we can well imagine, for we all know how she has been through her phychic and emotional proclivities made subject to these unholy bonds of death. And this, even this, is to our finding one of the greatest and most blessed fruits in our day of the triumph of the one great Labour-lover set forth so clearly, so potently for all who can see it in the life of Jesus the young carpenter of Nazareth.

☩ ☩ ☩

This applies to all who are vessels or via *media of the Word, and I give this now because of the need of many for this word of light in these days of sore proving.*

For the younger members of this our prophetic order, hearing the word speaking in them for the first time, and being not yet in the selfless Love, are very, very prone to imagine it to be so great a distinction to be thus used, that they naturally form an exaggerated opinion of their own importance, and get puffed up with all manner of self-vanities, and so are carried out of truth; whereas the maturer vessels, knowing the word of old, see all these things in their true proportions, and take them quietly, caring little now even to inquire carefully into them. For these things, occult or otherwise, are now part of their very being, and instead of studying them they seek to live them.

☩ ☩ ☩

And this leads me naturally to a kindred theme.

I have been asked by so many of the children of the new

Life concerning the recent return of many in the T. S. and elsewhere to the forms of the service of the old Catholic Church, that I take this opportunity of saying to my readers in a few words what I have already said publicly on many occasions.

I do not criticise, far less condemn, any of these my brethren in Christ for this return towards these things of the past, for I know too well the insatiable hunger of the spiritual nature for its own food.

This food can only pass through the channel of devotion or aspiration; for the way of its life is in the outgoing of love for the Beloved and in the incoming of love from the Beloved.

The artist or lover of beauty in us demands its food; and these devotional or aspirational forthgoings of the soul are all, even in their most crude or primitive expression, in this mode of the great love-song of nature.

And she, our own gentle psychè, must be satisfied in her aspirations or longings for Life.

Indeed, indeed as you, the lover of God, know so well, in the denying to her of this food is a far greater privation than in the denying to you of any other food of your nature.

Now we all know that in these merely intellectual, scientific, or occult societies no such food has been given, or can be given; nor have they professed to give it, for as a rule they work avowedly on the purely mental plane.

Therefore I can not only understand the hunger of these little children of the Christ-nature but I can sympathise with it, and that in no ordinary measure, even unto this truly human desire of the artist for the touch of beauty through the senses, for I too am an artist and a very child in the Christ-nature.

And, as already written in the Foreward to the Christ of the Holy Grail, we cannot deny the service of rite and of form for the little children, of whom some are yet so small and so feeble in their power of spiritual perception that these kindergarten methods are best for, even needful to them still.

Instead therefore of criticising, I would give for the service of these dear children of my own Christ, what to me has been for many years now, and becomes more and more an altogether satisfactory conception, perception, and realisation of the very present power of this near and real Presence that they so desire, and without which in very fact, and it is not too much to say, they feel that they can no longer live.

The good thing I give here is necessarily in fragmentary form, yet they who can find and take what is there involved and suggested, will find in this work, even as in most of my other works, hints towards the essentials of the great doctrine of the holy communion through all the elements of the one Body of God in Life.

A work given entirely to the love and service of this the great theme of my spiritual genius, and which has been forming itself in me for some years will be given you, my dear reader, in due time, if such is the will of the Giver.

✠ ✠ ✠

For the word is one and whole, even as God is one and whole; and it changeth never.

And the whole word for man has ever been uttered through the human soul; and it is found as it were, hid in all great scriptures. And that was the word for that day.

But its expression can only be according to the capacity of the vessel or efficiency of the channel through which it utters itself, and in this is its only limitation.

And even as this vessel is greater and more efficient to-day, inasmuch as the great human soul has gained in knowledge and in power spiritual, mental, and moral, so must the expression of the ageless Word be greater and fuller to-day than it was, say 2,000 years ago.

And this and not that is the Word of God for this day. And to utter this live word is the will, the joy, and the labour of your soul, my sister, my brother, and of my soul.

And on the life-page of the soul of the world, and on your life-page, and on my life-page, and on the life-page of every creature are written these scriptures. Yes, written with the very hand of God, and in the plenary inspiration of the One Holy Spirit of Life.

And manifold as are the types of our humanity so manifold are the modes of the great Christ-melody, the ageless Thing of Life, who sang its cosmic note as truly in the heart of the ancient pyramid as in St Peter's of Rome or St Paul's of London.

For this living word is the one ever-unfolding Beauty of God, even the holy Christ-Beauty that is ever becoming, and ever becoming more and more manifest as it passes through the untold ages of our human course.

And so we may say truly that this child of the unnumbered births who is now being brought forth for the regeneration and beautifying of the soul of to-day, even through you, my sister, my brother, dear in the service of Love, just as through me, must manifest more of the infinite Beauty than was possible to manifestation in the ages of the past.

For the Christ of the ages is one and whole, but the holy child now born of this living One in you and me is verily the child of the human need and of the human strength of to-day.

✠ ✠ ✠

Well, well it is when we have gathered into the One Beauty all our past spiritual goods.

Well, well when we can kneel with the little child who prays to Jesus, or Chrishna, or Hari, in as true a consciousness of the God-presence as when we sit in silence with the advanced initiate. It is well when we can worship as truly by the side of the Salvationist as of the Buddhist, by the side of the most ardent devotee of churchly form and rite as truly as by the strong and free-born son of the Spirit, whose shrine is the open light and the vast air of the lonely hillside or the deep shade of the pine forest, and who finds no name for the holy Presence of his days.

Yes, it is well, for we are now in the wholeness of the spiritual consciousness, and in every shrine of God is our home.

And all our own has come back to us.

And we know that we are in the one holy communion of heaven and earth.

And we know that all the spiritual consciousness of the past ages of our racial Body is ours.

And we know that her Life is our life, and that her labour is our labour, until all come into the Beauty of God.

And verily this it is to be in the power and blessing of the one and only Catholic Church of the Heaven and Earth of our race, the live and whole Body of God in our great creation.

☥ ☥ ☥

The form in which I offer this work to you, my dear reader, is somewhat of the nature of an experiment. All my writings are the fruit, more or less elaborated by my touch, of the one holy Power who works in and through me. This has ever been so, not only with my writings but with my public speaking.

But instead of working up and welding together into literary form these utterings of the inspiring one in me, I have left many of them very much as they came to me. And that I have done so is not a fruit of my human will as an artist but simply because I cannot well do otherwise in these days of our common travail.

Indeed, what I now give you is more or less of the nature of a mosaic of song. For these words are verily snatches of the Great Song as it sings itself in me, and all I have done as the artist is to try to give to them their natural sequence.

And I feel that they will yield their own individual virtues or powers more efficiently if I give them thus.

Consequently for any repetitions and apparent imperfections of form I have your indulgence.

But there may also be a good reason why I have so written. For I have found that, owing to the great strain of these years, people are not at present as fit as they were to follow any long or closely elaborated treatise, even had it been in the present use of my mental power so to treat these gentle mysteries of the Great Beauty.

And now, and now that we are called to sing again the song of the Healing Christ, which theme is ever to us the sweetest and best, we can say to our psychè after her travail of years: Return unto thy quiet rest, O my soul, for truly the Holy Lover hath led thee well and kept thee in the path of Blessedness even through all these days of our human woe. Turn thee, turn thee again unto the sweet pasture-lands of Life by the still-flowing, deep waters of the great peace.

A Call to the Children.

Little children of Christ, all of you, come to the call of the great Shepherd. For it is not my voice but the voice of the one Shepherd of souls who calls you now through the human love of this servant-laddie.

Come, all ye little ones of the flock of Christ, come unto the comfort of the many, many folds in the garment of Love.

Come unto the Bosom of the one holy Lover, who is the Mother and the Father of all men and all creatures.

Come, all of ye; for whether ye be German or Briton, or Turk or Armenian, or Russian or Austrian, or Jew or Gentile, ye are children of the One Lover.

Come ye then and drink now of the milk of the compassion of the Mother and the Father in God, and bring no money wherewith to buy for it is beyond all price.

For the gentle Lover knows and loves ye well, all of you, ay, loves ye well, even because of your uncleannesses, diseases, weaknesses and sins.

And there is not one of you, howsoever black and vile ye appear to your own eyes and to the eyes of man to be, who is not the child of Christ, your own Mother and Father and Lover in God.

For ye are all, all, all of you in the heart of God, and not one of you can ever be away from that love-centre of your one common life.

For this, this is your ageless Home; and ye can never be away from this Home. And no soul in whom the Eye of light shines, and no life in whom God's breath is breathing can ever be lost unto God.

Hear then ye little children of the Mother and the Father, the Saviour and the Healer, hear the calling of the wee herd-laddie; for he is calling to you out of the heart of the Good Shepherd.

And in his love of you is the Love of the Great Lover

of man and every creature; and in his calling is the calling of the Christ of your own nature; and this is the burden of his song as He the Man-lover, the living Sun of the aspiring power in you calls unto Her the sweet and bonnie dearie of your nature, the Jesus-woman in you who is ever from the glen suspiring towards the sunlit heights of the hill of God.

" *Ca' the ewes tae the knowes,*
Ca' them whaur the heather grows,
Ca' them whaur the burnie rows,
My bonnie dearie."

To the Spiritual Soul of the one holy catholic Church of Christ on earth.

(We have all testified that the power of the new Thing of Life is coming out of the trenches, even as, according to the law of our human economy, all power for good is generated in and must be found in hell.)

Awake, awake, O ageless bride of the great Lover of man, awake out of thy long sleep and clothe thee now in the fair robe thy Lover hath made ready for thee.

For behold, it is a fairer and more costly robe than any of those heretofore woven for thee by thy Lover.

And if only thou canst see its beauty and feel its price thou wilt no longer be able to cling to the worn-out rags that so many in thee still dream to be the live Body of the Lord of Life.

For surely of a priceless cost is this new robe, being woven and dyed by the Hand of thy Lover out of the live flesh and blood, out of the very heart and soul of the unnumbered martyrs of the ages to the truth of Holy Love, and notably in these days of our great deliverance, out of the very life-tissue and live substance of these myriads of innocent youths of our and other lands whom, through these long years of our world-agony, our eyes have been made to look on as the lambs without blemish, led—voluntarily and involuntarily—to the great sacrifice of the victims of our iniquity of lust and greed and its hell-born progeny of lies and hates.

To all you of all peoples is our call to the enrobing of the new and greater righteousness. For of a truth the robe is ready, ready even now, and only awaits your will to clothe you in its folds of power.

✠ ✠ ✠

For the good Mother has told me that her children are of all the peoples and of all the varieties of thoughts and feelings and even of ethics found in our human family.

And she has told me plainly that all these peoples have to learn from one another, and have to give freely of their own peculiar good to one another

Thus have I been told that Christianity and Buddhism are mutually serviceful, and have much of a good and a real use to give to one another, and that this will actually be realised in the world-wide mode of the great Christ utterance that is about to be.

For as we all must see, nothing can be more alien to the very genius of this Holy Body of God on earth as in the super- or sub-mundane worlds than to limit it to any time or degree or dispensation or mode of human expression.

And so all creeds, institutions, systems pass, but the Holy One, the Indwelling Presence abideth ever, ay, the Weaver and the Wearer of the robe abideth ever. And blessed are they who know that their home is in the Holy One of the Ages of our race. For let every temporary resting-place of a churchly or communal or personal nature be taken from their enjoyment, as in good time it surely will, yet abides sure and unfailing their eternal dwelling-place. And nevermore, ay, nevermore can the soul who has once found God be without an abiding. For Christ is God to them, and this Holy Presence is their own ageless and eternal, ever-abiding and never passing Home of Comfort.

The Offering of our Fragrance to the White Rose of the Island of the New Life.

O Christ, Thou bonnie, bonnie Child,
All day Thy songs sing in me;
All thro' the night, in fragrance wild,
Thy holy joys spring in me.
(See "Out of the Mouths of Babes.")

THE labours of body and soul and mind had been many and intense during these months in the south, and I had to betake me once more to the toning and invigorating powers of the All-father in the strong salt airs of my island, and to the sweetening, rehumanizing, enriching, and re-creating powers of the All-mother in the play of the little children in the home of the clean diet and the holy love over there in Liverpool.

I have already told you quite enough about this home in "Out of the Mouths of Babes," but as the island is equally a gift of the Great Lover to my nature at this time, I feel I should tell you just a little about it. It lies out on the sands o' Dee, about a mile from the Cheshire coast, and it looks right over to the hills and green braes of North Wales.

For twice four hours every day it is completely surrounded by the sea, and so my little game for years has been to land here just in time to be surrounded by the inflowing tide, and thus to be left for a good four hours alone with the sea birds and my other friends, visible and invisible, of the sea and the sun, the winds and the rains.

During these ten days we have been favoured with very hot sunshine, and so I have been able to indulge in my very ancient pastime of the alternate sea-bathe and sun-bathe; for it is well that the sea-bathe goes first.

(In this frequent dip, rub and sun-bath there is a greater, and I find, more pleasant service of health than in the usual one long bathe.

And I can have it here any fine day. For when the tide is too far out for the kiss of the great Maria, my body finds it as sweet and as pure in a bath that my own good Mother has carved for me out of the living rock.

She has made it just wide enough for my body and deep enough for it to be utterly submerged. And here too, and just where they should be, are two arms wherein I can stretch my hands fully and no more, for their bath.

Thus, you see, it is in the form of a live cross, and so I greatly love to bathe therein among my little fishes. Indeed I so love it, that, though it lies full two hundred paces over the rocks, I gladly face a north-easter to get to it.

And the bed is of green moss floating on white sand, where, by way of a little fun, the playful sea-nymphs have sown some bonnie shells!

Really, really though she appear "red in tooth and claw," she is the Great Mother, and in all her ways, ay, even in them all I say, she plays, she plays, if only we have eyes to see it, she plays with her little children.)

Now this is one of those scenes in holy nature that the artist never ventures to profane by trying to describe, for he knows that it is best seen when left to the imagination. So I'll only tell you that I am now back in London, writing you this at dawn in a body that has been most thoroughly re-vitalized in this twofold baptism of water and fire, and that has clothed itself in a new, clean, well-toned skin, having shed, even as does the wise serpent, the old skin, which, as many of you know, is a simple process of peeling by the power of the sun. And, like all the processes of divestation, it is good, good and only good, even though it causes certain discomforts to this old animal nature.

Now my island clothes herself, just as all ladies do, and do rightly, in robes of beauty that vary in colour according to the seasons.

She had been decked in early spring with the living green of the sweet, young grass; now she is wearing out her magnificent, full-spring, glory-costume of golden dandelions, many of which have still enough of sweet juice in their pipes to tempt my appetite towards that most wholesome, nourishing, and cleansing tonic; and she is just bringing forth her finest early summer frock of the white rose.

This frock is so very delicate a frou-frou that it wears only for two or three weeks, and then she will take to herself her long-enduring summer robe of the hardy pink sea-daisy, the wild golden clover, the cup of yellow gold, and, latest of all, the bonnie purple heath followed by her brother, the chaste and hardier heather of my own Bens.

So now, as we are cosily tucked amid the folds of her white-rose frock, we shall just give you a little of our feeling of its beauty, for some of you do not know it.

It is the first really sweet-smelling, fragrant, living thing of glory that our earth produces on the land that has been rested, cleansed, and fed well by the strengths of the salt Maria, and then redeemed by the power of the sun from the barrenness which is hers without his kiss.

And for this very reason it is the finest, purest, least earthy of all the flowers I know, whether in scent, in bloom, or in leaf.

For the genesis of this exquisite soul and body of beauty is on this wise: First, the earth-mother grows on the land that is being thus redeemed from barrenness, a strong, grassy tuft. This is the first green thing that appears on the sands from which the sea is withdrawing her waves.

Then, as soon as these grasses have prepared a soil fit to nourish their life, various bonnie wee mosses, bed-rocks, wild clovers, thymes, and other lowly creatures of wondrous colour come forth.

*And then, as though the sweet-scented and hardly visible **thyme** had effaced herself on purpose, there appears the white rose of the sand-hills, the first living thing of a great and fragrant glory.*

✣ ✣ ✣

Now it is even so with this holy thing, this Jesus Lovelight of to-day, this hidden joy of the heart.

For to my tasting it is verily the first utterly sweet and fragrant thing of glory that the Hand of the great Beauty has brought forth out of the abyssmal ocean of the ages of our earth's woes, and, to us the children of her sorrow notably so, out of these three years of the supreme agony of her travail.

And behold, behold, behold, all ye who have eyes to see, behold the Child, the Holy Love-child, has been born even in and through you and me, human soul, for her health and fuller life, and for the salvation of all her children.

And they who have tasted its sweetness know that it is the finest, the purest, the least earthy soul they have as yet tasted.

And so we call it the White Rose of the Island of Life.

✠ ✠ ✠

And under its blossom hid there, warm and comfie in her lowly nest, broods the mother-lark over her five bonnie brown eggs.

She has become so tame that she allows me to lie beside her and talk to her while the dear little daddy sings and sings his joy, high, high over us.

Yes, yes, it is ever so. The gentle, lowly creatures of this earth-life, whether it be soul of man or bird, seek the shelter of and find rest under the shadowing of the Great Love, whose finest beauty is seen in this one White Rose of the soul of Man, who is the will to bless, the desire to heal, the power to give life, even the unfailing, deathless urge in you, human soul, and in me, to cheer, to comfort, and to make beautiful everybody, every soul we can so serve.

"Jesus from the ground suspires."
(*Omar Khayyam*).

Are you able, dear child of Light, to come with me into the essence of the blessèd Christ, the Sun of our whole cosmos personal and universal, and to find the very soul of His sweetness, the power of His radiance in this one holy Thing of Life, this gentle creation of the divine love and wisdom?

☦ ☦ ☦

For indeed I find this fragrance known among men as the "Gentle Jesus" spirit, to be the essential, quintessential, ay, superessential process of the human substance, physical, psychic or mental and spiritual. Yes, I find it to be the strength of her soul and the life-bouquet of our humanity, the holy thing of our nature, her power of the supreme refining, even the very perfume of God in man.

And as in the whole nature and life of man, so in the whole nature and life of Demeter, the mother of animal-man, the earth-born heir of heaven, of man the child of God.

All the virtues, sweetnesses, vital powers and strengths of the winds and the rains, the snows and the frosts, the raging storms and the serene calms of ocean, of high mountain, great forest and wide plain, the balmy airs of their night and the live heat of their noon, the great warmth of their summers and the rigid cold of their winters, the consuming heat of the sun and the comforting of his quiet and voiceless radiance, the virtues of the soul of all the live creatures of our earth, human and sub-human, animal and elemental, the beauty and gentle services of all sweet-smelling flowers and all healing plants, of all the beasts of the earth, birds of the air and fish of the sea, all, all, all I find in this one Divine sweetness of God we name "Jesus." And this I find to be the all-essential, never-failing holy thing of power in all healing and in all modes.

☦ ☦ ☦

This is the holy thing of power that can and will shed, ay, that verily loves to shed, and cannot be truly satisfied in its desire of love, until it has shed its very finest bouquet, its most choice sweetness over the hand that wounds and the heart that loves to wound in the most exquisite of pains your tenderest parts of flesh or soul or mind, the power of love that can even make you strong enough in God that it be as nothing for you to lay the glory of your head and the beauty and the pride of your life beneath the foot of the mind who knows best how, and of the will who most effectively oppresses, tortures or afflicts your human nature.

☩ ☩ ☩

And supremely, distinctly, and above and beyond all in our incarnate experience, it is surely the holy love-sweetness of the bonnie, bonnie new-born Christ Child, blossoming, shedding its beauty and yielding its ageless, deathless fruit through these live vessels of the Christ-body of our ascension as a race into the higher and fuller life-consciousness of the super-material.

For there as here it is verily the fine bouquet of the essence of the present refining of our higher, our fairer, our nobler, our greater humanity.

And well we know from our life-long and most intimate experience, that in no mode of its self-giving movement is it more exquisitely sweet than when it comes to us through the live and near and real presence of the arisen belovèd. For then indeed its sweetness is more than our or any words of earth-sound can tell.

It is of such a quality that it can only be uttered in the tears of an unbounded, immeasurable and inexpressible blessedness.

☩ ☩ ☩

For they have now become "Jesus" in real essence as in actual existence, being one in spirit, one in nature, one in power and function, and one in activity with this cosmic, catholic, whole and holy substance of the genus man, and out of this primal, virginal, eternal, ageless, ever verdant and fecund ground in the Christ-body of our humanity, they breathe, ever breathe forth for the sweetening, purifying and vitalizing of all our personal and social atmospheres or conditions of flesh or of mind, of will or of soul, the sweet perfumes and holy breaths, strong, strong in the health of God, of the ever-green hills and never-withering plants and fruits and flowers and of all the pure creatures of this our own and true homeland.

They are now in and of the very body or build of the Holy Grail of God, even the live vessel of the one Christ of all men and all ages of our race. And in this supreme fact of the history of man as an evolving soul of the service of life universal I find the great, primal and never-failing, mediational source of all our power.

☦ ☦ ☦

And I repeat, for it is worthy, this we know and testify to be so, because we, even we have in these days, even these latter days of this dispensation, been fed, beautified, quickened, ay, glorified in our personal nature thereon, through the holy vessel of the little one, the new-born and arisen child of Christ.

☦ ☦ ☦

O, human soul, what a holy vessel of God art thou! what a beauty can shine in and through thee as the Grail of Life!

Surely, surely, it is well worth all the labours and pains of the one Potter's working in thee throughout all these ages of thy manifold existences, to have brought thee unto the state wherein thou canst be the worthy vessel, receiver or reservoir, channel and giver to drink of this Divine sweetness, brewed out of the love-blood of the heart, as the drink and food of the little ones of thy Father-Mother Christ, even of every creature of earth, human and sub-human, who can receive the good service of thy love.

✠ ✠ ✠

I was walking early this morning near Bingley in a neighbourhood entirely new to me.

The Sun of my nature was shining forth clearly and strongly; and his radiance fell on two little children.

One of these, a tot of not more than 5, ragged and unwashed indeed, yet a veritable picture of health and beauty, soon as she saw me simply rushed into my arms.

When she and her companion had received the kiss and the hug of love and were moving away, I overheard the little one say: "It's God." No, said the other after a pause: "It's Jesus."

And here once again, out of the mouths of babes the word of truth has been given to me, as to every lover of the child.

For we can give "God" and we can be "Jesus" to one another if we will to be so. And I ask you now brother, sister in Life: Do you give God, are you as Jesus to any human soul? Do you radiate the light, do you breathe forth the sweetness of love to any soul? If not, know this to be the truth of your nature: You can, you can, you can if only you will, ay, if only you will.

Yes, even to-day, even at this hour you can be, if you will to be, the live vessel of the Divine blessedness.

The coming of the Jesus Child.

I cannot tell how, during these past years of our great human woe and travail of soul, circumstances have combined in the most near and dear relationships of my life to try, to search, and almost to crush this human soul.

Indeed, I can only express the fact by saying that I know that the most determined and subtle attacks were made on the very centre of my life and on the very citadel of my power of judgment by the adversary, or trier, through the use of these the most sensitive and vulnerable points of my nature.

And it had well-nigh succeeded; for a deep, deep sorrow and a dark and hopeless, and what was most unnatural to me, a pessimistic attitude of mind was surely gaining power in my soul.

One day, when these circumstances had come to a crisis, I was walking alone, in a grimy haze, on a lonely seashore, against a cold east wind. To all appearances things could not be worse than they were, and at the very end of myself, renouncing once and for all the effort of wit or of will to save me, I offered my life, ay, and my very soul, and all that I am, to the will of the old adversary of our blessedness.

And I did so, utterly, irrevocably, sanely, and I cried in the agony of this self-surrender: Never again shall I seek to avoid any evil, any pain, any sorrow. I shall go to the deepest of the abyss of suffering and I shall say to the crucifier: Now do your best on me. Henceforth I shall not care what its effect on my life may be.

And, lo, that very mid-night a new Thing was born in my soul, and the holy Love-light came into my consciousness in a way and in a measure never heretofore experienced by me, and it gave in me its name, and it called itself Jesus.

Now I had felt for some months that in my nature a holy Thing was in the process of becoming. There could be no doubt of this fact. And here was the simple forthcoming of the new Love. And this holy Child, this gentle Light of the smile of God, has been with me ever since, and has surely given me the good cheer of the ever present Power, even the Christ of our nature.

How well I know that for the actual preservation of my physical life from death this Love-child has come to abide in me.

For so great and potent was the above-noted combination of the most subtly destructive agencies that could be brought to work in the vitals of my present-day nature that I had given up all hope for the life of my body, and the power of sorrow was surely killing my flesh.

For this hoary thing, even sorrow, the besetting sin of the *Il penseroso* type of soul, has something to do with our very intensely artistic Gaelic temperament and seems to be about the last undesirable guest who is willing to quit this old house of our habitation!

Yet had she, even she the sallow-faced, to pass before the power of the all-conquering Sun of my nature. For the living one has already taken from me a very decided horror I had for the processes of the dissolution of the body—so intense an aversion that even when I saw a hearse approaching from afar I would turn my eyes away from it.

It has enabled me to say as above, and in the very real word of actual deed: I will not shrink from any unpleasant experience. I will go into the very worst, yea if need be, bear in this body the greatest pain or humiliation. And I will fear no evil.

Now for me whose whole nature shrank through and through from the grimy, the painful, the diseaseful, the sordid, the deformed, the ugly, it is indeed something to have been enabled to utter that word of the whole will, even the word of true liberation.

And I say again, I know well that it is the holy Indweller who has enabled me in any measure so to do.

Jesus the Light of the Love of God.

Now when I speak of Jesus I mean to convey to your mind a consciousness of the Light of the God-love. And to me this pure, ideal, superpersonal Essence is always uttered when I use this name.

But this use in no way implies that I deny the historical existence on our earth of a holy man, in whose personality this great beauty of God was realised and manifested.

Indeed, so far as my personal consciousness and realisation therein tells me, I distinctly feel that such an one was, and is even now a real human presence, working in the service of our human progress.

And yet to my seeing this is a non-essential absolutely and without qualification. For the Great Light is in the soul of the Race, and there, if we would find it, we must seek it ever, finding it ultimately and as an abiding reality within our own nature.

And the finer and truer my vision, the stronger and purer my love, the maturer, more beautiful my humanity becomes, so much the nearer and nearer do I get to the Jesus or holy Child in every soul.

And so much the more and more do I desire to become the Child, and, truth to tell, the more and more do I feel that I am a little child, cared for in all my ways and led by the good hand of the Mother and the Father in God.

And the Mother and the Father is your Christ and mine, and the good hand is the serving Angel of this holy Presence.*

---

* Verily we have no longer any vital interest in any question of any personality in the past.

What does concern us is the present, the living reality.

And this is why we search and search so diligently the holy scripture of God within our nature where alone we can discover the vital arcana of these things that so really matter.

For, of this we are at least as sure as we are of any truth (and we deny not the truth and service of the most ancient and great human doctrine of reincarnation), that, whether or no we associate the universally present Power of the healing Jesus-Love with the personality and history of a man who was once known as Jesus of Nazareth, is to this holy one as much a matter of indifference as I trow it is even now to me your brother to know whether I ever dwelt in the body of a Druid, of a Greek, or of an Egyptian!

For the forth-sending of the Holy One of your nature.

The distinction and unfailing characteristic of Love in all the degrees and modes of her manifestation is that she wills to serve, must serve, and ever serves.

And as in the outer so in the inner, as in the human so in the divine.

And thus the great Love is ever the servant of the lowliest soul who truly wills the blessing of the other, and fulfils the services of love for the sake of the other, and not for the sake of self.

This otherness is, as you know, a fundamental principle in the very being of white magic, and an essential principle in the power and use of this Christly thing.

For this is, and may well be named the great and holy Christ-magic; and there is no magic to compare with it in power.

Now this holy One may be known, and in many cases, possibly in all cases, is known to the soul in whom the great union is complete, by an intimate or personal name, it may be as Jesu the Lover, or Christ the living sun, or the gentle Buddha of the holy light, or Krishna the blissful, Krishna of the magic flute.

Many are the names or expressions of this universal Blessedness, and it matters not what the name given you may be, for this name is for the use of your nature, and is related to your temperament, time and place of birth, education and other temporalities.

Therefore, in the use of the following word of promission it may be well, if so be that you have found or need a personal name, to substitute another name for any one I give.

Surely, surely, when we have used and laid aside these old and worn-out garmentings, we have done with them once and for all. Surely, surely, in this also the wisdom of the Christ-word in us is great in its health:—Let the dead bury their dead, and come thou with me into Life.

And though in you it may not be known by any personal name, yet is this holy and most intimate Presence there, even in you who love; and in the name of Love you can send it forth, and it will not fail, I surely trow, to fulfil the prayer of your will or the desire of your self-giving love. *(See Word of Promission, p. 99.)*

The Coming of the Holy One of Healing.

Now this Holy One comes unto our desire out of the unfathomed deep of God. Not that we consciously or wilfully call it forth.

But when the whole nature is in the great stillness of the selfhood, the Holy Thing comes forth of its own will out of the deep of God within the soul, and meets us there as friend meets friend, face to face and eye to eye. And there is no contact more real, more intimate, more personal than this contact.

And when it is so it is sufficient to name such and such an one; for, while you are in this deep and vital conscious contact, the thought of such an one brings it into the same contact of blessing.

Thus, whether named or not, they who are to be served through you come to you at the time, and are blessed in this touch of your own living God. And when this union has been fulfilled in your innermost consciousness, and the Holy One has become you, volitionally, psychically, mentally, spiritually for the time, you can send it forth as your temperamentally qualified power of blessing unto all, all, all who can then be served through your personal nature.

And this is the great forthsending of the living Christ, symbolized in the eucharistic service of the mass, and expressed in the words; *missa est, i.e.,* it is sent.

Concerning this most holy union and communion there is much to say that I cannot say. But this I can say to you here, that in my very body I have experienced what I know to correspond in the inner degree of our nature to the experiences of the fecundation of the womb of life; for the woman in me has certainly known that this is so.

The Light of Reason in the Healer.

The spiritual healer always works in the Reason of things and in the Light of truth.

Therefore it is that if a call for service comes to you as a healer, there will always be a good reason for that call and a sure need for that service.

And you will know exactly what to do and how to do it.

And the more persistent and insistent this call, the greater is the need and the surer is the fruition of health through your service in that soul or body.

Herein the sacredness of the call, and so sacred is it realised to be by those who are in the light of the knowledge that they must do all in their power at any time and in any circumstances to fulfil the call.

The Divestation of Love.

Even as the heat of the sun as it increases day by day causes us to throw off garment after garment until at last we wear nothing that we can do without, so the power of the Great Love, even the heat and radiance of the One Living Sun, makes us willing, and at last even eager, to divest ourselves of all the garmentings of our animal and psychic selfhood, wherein, for its protection during the periods of the embryonic and other early stages of growth, our kind mother in God, holy nature, had swaddled and clothed the God-child of our being.

And it follows as a sure fruition that the more our spiritual soul is thus divested, the finer, sweeter, and fuller is her appreciation of the power and will of the Great Love thus aworking for her larger life and greater blessedness.

And this process of unclothing and the consequent increasing sensitiveness goes on and on until at last, as we have every reason to believe and affirm, the Holy Atma, the blessed Love-Light, the "gentle Jesus" of this human soul, is one in consciousness and in all the forthgoings of its life with the one Blessedness who filleth all and is in all.

✠ ✠ ✠

Now, even as Jesus, through the utter yielding-up of his nature to the great liberating power of the all-dissolving Essence, whereby the elements of his personal selfhood were set free, entered into the greater Life-consciousness and became the pure spirit who could be in any number of places, souls, works or experiences at the same time, and could inspire this one here and that one there, even unto an unlimited number (and in manifold ways or modes) at the same time; and actually did so, using for this purpose as at Pentecost, both the discarnate and incarnate media who were suited temperamentally to one another, so now this same Christ-essence or spirit may so work its good work of liberation in you and in me, that we too become pure spirit, ubiquitous, free from the limitations of this degree, able to be wherever the service calls us, and having the power to fulfil the desire of our will.

The Blood of Jesus.

You know what it is, O sensitive, feeble, weary, human soul, to suffer, and suffer, and suffer in the most utter and exquisite modes of pain because of the errors either of your own present or past, or of that of others. And the more sensitive to feel and the more righteous in will you become while in this mode of service the more you suffer thus.

And though I speak here of this special mode of the great suffering service, be it well understood that all the good I now deduce therefrom can be equally deduced from any other of the many modes of the suffering service of these the finest vessels of our race.

We all know our own past, and some of us, because of temperamental intensities, richnesses, and other possibilities in our nature, have been greater "sinners" than others, at least from the ordinary worldly view-point, in having through error of judgment apparently just missed the mark in failing to do "the right thing."

And in as much, and in exact proportion as we are sensitive, kindly natures, this will have brought us much and intense suffering, and this suffering works in us as a fermenting of the very elements of our nature, and this process of ferment, and brewing may continue for days, or months, or even years, at a time.

Now it may be, and it is very likely, that we have in past days fled, as for very life's sake, from, and used all manner of means to cover or hide us from such suffering, even as from all kinds of suffering. And this is because we were not yet strong enough to bear the pain and so fulfil the service.

But a time has at length come when we have been able to say:—I shall no longer flee from this. I shall henceforth yield my whole nature up to its power. I shall allow it to do all its will in me.

And you have deliberately given your cheek to the smiter and your live flesh to the scourger.

And you have taken it all quietly, not uttering one word of complaint, either to your own or to any other soul incarnate or decarnate.

In fact you have jealously guarded her against seeking any sympathy, either from herself or from any other soul, for instinctively you have felt that just in as much as you have yielded to self-pity, or secured the pity of any other soul, you have lost for the use of your nature something that is more precious to her than can be computed by the ordinary judgment on values.

And here, as in all else, what I speak of as the instinct of your forthcoming nature, will prove itself true, and will not fail to guide you in the way of this unfolding life.

For in very fact you have interfered with the process of the distilling of a something that is priceless as the very elixir of the soul of our creation.

And this something is the essential power of Life, for it enables you to endure in love and to be still in all your elements, so that God may be allowed to work in and through you the great work of the transmutation of the stuffs of the great animal soul of the race.

And every time we allow the self-preserving instinct of the blind self-love of the old animal nature thus to utter itself in us we shall in the same way interfere with the great work of the new life in our nature.

And every time we allow the self-transcending love to work in us we shall surely find that it is even as we have just said.

And this sure law of the new life can never fail, and so it is even now; and you, even you, O sensitive, feeble, weary, human soul, will now see and reap and taste the first fruit of the new blessedness arising within you.

For, behold, in the fulness of time, out of this experience has come forth a more tender tenderness, a greater compassion, a sweeter, a gentler, a holier love for all, all, all whosoever, wheresover, or whatsover, they be. And this, even this, is the sure fruition of this work, and you will never find it to fail.

Now you are the knower, and the only human knower and judge of your own soul, and if there is anything you do know you know that this is so.

And you also know instinctively that in this more intense power of love is the very essence or strength of the new Life; that it is the one and only all-cleansing, all-vivifying reality thereof.

And in like manner you also know that through you, even you, human soul, whoever you be, it is distilled for all; and is of a very and absolute necessity of its divine nature, given to all in all the realms of need in our human cosmos.

And you know further, and this from well-observed facts in your daily life, that this holy thing who is thus brought forth in and through your soul is indeed the absolute and one essential beauty of God in and for our human degree, even the Great Beauty, in whom is the healing and the health, the vivifying and renewing, the onward, ever onward power in the march of the race.

And even though the robustness of the animal nature and the beauty of the physical may be so entirely drawn into the use of this all-absorbing power that your very form is marred thereby to the eye of fleshly beauty, you will find that in the gentler thing thus brought forth in you is a finer tenacity of Life, a more vital beauty even of personality, and above all, and as the best that you can give to the needy soul of the world, the never-failing peace, the peace of God, even the live word of the whole harmony of Life, shedding itself in and through every mode or expression of your everyday being.

For, once thy soul, my brother, my sister in Christ, hath indeed said by the word of the full consent of thy whole nature: I am willing, O Christ, to be pierced with all the wounds of thy body; willing, willing that my life be poured forth for the bearing away of the sin of the world, the great work of the refiner and transmitter of the elements has borne its fruit in your nature, and you may be very sure that the offering is already received of Love, and that thy life-stream, even the warm blood of thy heart-love and the sweet water of thy soul-life, will be received in the holy Grail of the Christ of Healing and there used for the cleansing and healing of the soul of the world.

And you will not be in any way dismayed when you find that you are being pierced through and through your most sensitive parts, for you will then know well that these are the wounds of the body of the Lamb of God in your nature.

Surely, surely then, dear human soul, whoever you be, when you know that this is even as I have now said, you will be more and more willing, wheresoever and whatsoever be the circumstances thereof, to endure all, all, all that you may be henceforth privileged to bear for the great work of the cleansing, vitalising, and beautifying of the soul of the world.

And your brother knows that in this he has spoken to you the holy truth, and he gives it to you now for the comfort and strengthening of the suffering Christ of your human nature.

And because he knows so many of these most gentle souls suffer through their regrets, this word is given for their special comfort, so that they may see that even these regrets, while in no way to be fosterd or encouraged but rather discountenanced through and through, are nevertheless used, as are all the expressions of Life commonly named " evil," for their abiding good.

Herein is the great mystery of the service of Love in our present estate, and it is the service of the cross of the Christ of our nature.

Concerning the Jesus-Christ of our nature.

Now it comes to me, and very clear is the apprehension in the Light that " the Christ" is the one great fructifying power of our spiritual and material, personal and solar cosmos, the essential and actual source of the power of physical generation that radiates through the soul and body of our earth's sun, even as through our soul and body, who has been working the great work even in my nature as the enrichener and quickener, refiner and beautifier during these long ages, and that this Jesus-presence is the fine and ripe fruit of this work within my new psyche or spiritual nature, the very love-child of God in me, who has been fed and made strong to do its work of blessing in my nature through the nutritional, age-long blessing of its own one Father-Mother, the Great Christ of our cosmos, and in the fulness of time has come forth, a whole creation of the love of the great Beauty, complete in all power to be the Saviour, the Redeemer, the Unifier of this human soul of very crude, very mingled, very strong, and very difficult elements.

For this holy Presence in me is one with the great love-principle, and its coming is ever identified in my experience with the coming or arising within of the one and only power that has indeed made life, in any sense of the word, a joy or even liveable to me, even the holy Thing we name Love.

Or, if you will, let us express it thus, for indeed the utterings or modes of expression of this twain Blessedness are manifold as are the services of the Beauty of God, and correspond in all ways, details, and degrees thereto, that the Jesus manifests in us more of the feminine of the great Beauty, even what to us is the gentle, woman-love, who can and will enter into our personal wants and cares, trials and labours, ever nourishing, protecting, and comforting us in all respects, whereas the Christ manifests more of the masculine who, as the living Sun of our nature, inspires, illumines, directs, and rules over all the powers or planets of the cosmos of our being.

And the whole of God in us would thus be the Two in One, named in our western speech Jesus-Christ, the holy Twain, the Father and Mother, the Lord and Lover, the Master and Servant, even the Comforter and Friend of all our days, whose great and universally human name for us is Love.

And we find it is so, and even as the unifying of our nature progresses so is it manifest. For there is no one so near and familiar to you, human soul, as is this holy Lover.

Indeed, nothing could be more intimately personal than the modes of its service. Thus, *e.g.*, have you any way to go which might be peculiarly trying to your nature? You are sure to find the Friend waiting there to accompany you through that dark passage. "For lo, I am with thee yea in thee always, the rod and the staff of my presence staying thee, comforting thee, O human soul, through whatever shade thy path may pass."

How the Presence serves all the needs of our nature.

And so it is that we can call on the Presence for the service of the health of any part or function of the body at any time and in any circumstance, howsoever lowly that part or function may appear to be in the order of our life, and howsoever inopportune may appear to be the time or the circumstances for this service.

Thus to illustrate: Some twelve years ago my heart was condemned as an organ of life by the first London "heart-specialists." Since then, however, I have done the best work of my life. Still, the old steed is a bit fiery, and wills to go a bit too keen at times!

And so, during these years the heart has often told me that I am not holding the reins as I ought to by apparently stopping to beat, the consequence of which is a very funny, but not at all unpleasant, feeling of being in another state, and, at times, even the complete faint. Well, within this past year of blessing, it has come naturally to me to say to my own, my near one, when that funny feeling was just coming on, using the most familiar and endearing term possible to our human speech: "Now, this is your job, and I leave it to you, my own dear one, to attend to my heart, and I know you will look after it all right."

And I now declare that sure as I have done so the feeling has always passed, and not once have I had these faints, which indeed had become too common for the comfort of my friends.

☩   ☩   ☩

For, to resume our theme, as you know, this operation may well be described as the merging of the inner and the outer: or the absorption of the lower self into the higher self, even the assumption of the Mary of our human nature into God. And when this is so, we know that we indeed come into all our own, for in this great work, as in all else, so perfect is the economy of Love that whatever of good may have been ours in the personal relationships of past lives, now enters into our own most intimate fellowship.

Thus do we lose none or nothing of the powers of service psychic or physical for healing or blessing in any way, that we may have won through service or attained to through any discipline of mind or soul or flesh in past lives or during this incarnation.

And even though we may now function on a plane that does transcend the physical or magnetic, yet do we recognise and use these modes of service soon as a call for such arises.

For this holy One is the very substance or home-principle of every soul, and is thus the unifying power in us all communally or socially as truly as individually.

And it is the innate, deathless, never-ceasing urge in

the human genius that keeps it seeking, and ever seeking for its true Self.

Thus she cannot but seek after the one living God in whom alone is her eternal rest.

Indeed, indeed, were it not of an indestructible, never-failing, all-subduing nature, it would not continue as it does to exist, far less to constrain its growth in its passage of redemption through the very mingled stuffs and indescribably crude conditions of the elements of our ancient nature.

The Holy Will of Life.

For, let us ask here as well *à propos*, what is this unceasing urge in us to do the good—this unwearying, undying will in us to serve and to bless; what is it but this holy Thing of Life or Love, manifesting oftimes so strangely, so imperfectly because of the limitations of our human nature, yet, yet, ever leading this nature towards the higher and the better, ever seeking to manifest through her the will of blessing?

✠ ✠ ✠

Yes, our holy One it is who ever sings in us the song of Life and the hymn of the great Joy, thus using all these powers temperamental and otherwise of our mingled nature; and if these powers are so used we are indeed blessed.

Who knows better than your brother how mingled the quality of this personal nature is; and yet I know that this man, ay, even this man here has been so used?

For this holy Love-light is the energising, enriching, fecundating power of God in the soul, and it manifests thus in the body through all the expressions of our life, even unto the very *timbre* of the voice, which becomes vibrant and strong, sweet and penetrating, vital and rich in the power of the health of the deathless, ageless, living Spirit.

Surely, surely in the sweet fellowship of these little children of the poor of our land, to which this holy Lover has admitted me, I have well proved during these maturer years of my life how real and true in very fact is the power of this live Presence.

For I do know that through these undefiled vessels this Presence of the Jesus-love comes, even this holy Thing, which, as I must so often declare, is to my finding the sweetest, the best that through the power of the one live Sun of our cosmos, our mother-earth has as yet conceived and brought forth through the travail of her whole nature: and never does my pipe sound forth more clearly than when I sing with them the child hymns of their Jesus-lover.

✠ ✠ ✠

And, need we say now for the service of her present need, that this is the power whose vision all through this great conflict of our world-forces has never wavered nor failed to show us clearly that the only way of an enduring peace is through Love.

And whether we be in the form of male or female, this one divine Jesus-woman in us, the holy Love-wisdom, ever utters through us the word of health and of the most practical use when we human vessels truly will it so.

And because to us She is always of the feminine principle, we feel that through the vessel of the great motherhood of man in the woman of to-day, must come forth *par excellence* the actual realisation of this one and only power of a world peace.

And this our finding has been well confirmed by the response of the true, sane, womanly woman of to-day to all our appeals to this one power of Life in Her, the mother for the liberation of her children from the thrall of greed, the delusions of self-interest, and the hell of hate.

✠ ✠ ✠

And our great labour is for the bringing forth of this great and fecund Beauty of God in the woman of to-day. And no pain so pierces our nature as to witness in any way the degradation or prostitution of this holy vessel of our humanity's good. And alas, alas, we are made, ay compelled through circumstances to be year-long witnesses of her sore and vile degradation.

The sweetness of the Jesus-presence and its power of Healing.

We all know not a few human presences whose aura and emanation, whether physical or psychic, may well be described as a sweet influence. The occultist would speak of it as a sweet magnetism.

It is so sweet that, once tasted, there is nothing you desire more.

These presences are the finest of our kind, our firstborn; and they are the best healers incarnate.

Now the quality of sweetness has, above all others, been usually applied by the little child as by the nature mystic saint to the Jesus-presence, and there is certainly a good reason for this as for all such facts of human consciousness.

And I feel that through my personal experience I have found for you, human soul, at least somewhat of this reason.

For when fulfilling the service of healing, whether by the service of the hand or physical presence or not, through the use of this name—and this name, be it well noted, never comes to me but as a sure indication from the one true recorder in my nature that the Presence is actually in me as the worker, the fact which is then most real to my perception is the sense of the sweetness of the Presence.

And this human word, and this word alone, can then

utter for me what is the only, the all-else-absorbing, the all-else-effacing consciousness.

And just in as much as this perception and actual tasting of the sweetness is intensified in my consciousness, in so much is the power of the Healer manifest in fruition.

Jesus the Healer.

I know that this Holy One is the Healer within me.

I have just been fulfilling what has been a favourite service with me for years now.

While the little ones are asleep in the early dawn I lie down beside one of them, this morning it was our bonnie, well-favoured Arthur, and I fulfil the silent service of healing there in their presence.

In this aura of a pure innocence the Jesus-healer is to my finding just at its best.

And it is indeed of a wondrous sweetness thus to go forth or to send it forth on the wings of these little ones' auric body simply by uttering and continuing to utter the name of Jesus.

Concerning the Jesus-presence.

So very sacred is this holy Thing to me that it is with difficulty I can speak of it in company, and I am able to do so only when those present are of the understanding heart.

Now, I do not, as I have so often said, deny the power of this holy presence for the service of any devout soul who looks to it in the ordinary way of a simple and pure devotion, as pertaining to something that happened in our world's history some 2,000 years ago, for I know that in such an apprehension is a real service to that soul, and I would be the last to take from it this good thing.

For this same Jesus personality is the very expression in the language of this simple-hearted Christian for the best of God; and all the best that can come to it comes at it thus.

And I know that it is the same holy One, even yours ond mine, who comes to the soul of my young brother while he hears the word of Life through some untutored Salvationist; and it is sweet to know that it is so.

But I must say that as soon as the ordinary literal or historical element is doctrinally introduced by any friend into this service of Life it has always lost for me its virtue or power of blessing; and only through the hymn of the little child has a breath of this power or beauty come to me, for thus it still abides and operates in its true place of power, even the realm of the ideal.

And this is the experience of many of my most spiritual companions who know Christ, not after the flesh but after the spirit, and to whom it is now a matter of no vital import whatsover whether the Jesus of the Gospels ever lived on earth or no; and I would ask you to allow me to say here that until this is so in our spiritual experience we have not found the Christ who can never be taken from us.

Yet, as I told you years ago in the Christ of the Holy Grail, I have had enough of occult experiences of the most reliable nature to satisfy me that the one known in history as Jesus of Nazareth is, as a real personality, very, very much even now in the service of our human need; and while I feel in that degree of my nature where such feeling is indeed the surest knowledge that in all this the same live personality verily, verily is, yet I also feel that there is more here than could pertain to any mere human personality. *(See Addenda p. 111.)*

For to me God, and all that word implies, comes in and with this great and gentle presence.

✠ ✠ ✠

Yes, I am very sure that this is no mere human spirit, intensely, beautifully human though it be in very truth, but a divine influence of an order who transcends the realm of all personal limitations, for it comes forth into my consciousness in the same way as a thought or spiritual inspiration arises, *i.e.*, as being innately and essentially of my own very soul, and having its abode even in my nature.

I know well, and fully appreciate the sensation of the coming of a discarnate spirit to make itself known in my consciousness, but this is certainly other and more than that.

For that is of the nature of a visitation, a clear coming in and a going away, but this is as the uprising or the forth-showing of the presence of a guest who is ever in the house, and whom you know to be always there, even as one who belongs to the home.

For the great good for you and me, human soul, to come unto through the age-long pilgrimages of our unfolding nature, so far as I have yet been able to see, is even so to become a truly spiritual, ubiquitous, or cosmic presence or influence who works its work of blessing wheresoever, whensoever, and in whomsoever it is called upon to serve in life.

And this is what I find the Jesus-presence to be, and in a degree surpassing all such influence known to me.

And where he, the Leader of our Life has come, you and I, human soul, will surely yet come ; and there is no experience or discipline of our days, how painful soever it be, for which we can be too thankful, for it all helps us on, enabling us to follow the one who was made perfect through suffering.

This is verily God to Me.

For this is verily God to me, ay, God become more near, more familiar, more real in presence and contact than that of any human soul.

And so I can declare to you, my reader, that in this most real and satisfying mode of consciousness I do know God even as God is, in essence and in substance, in the personal and in the universal, in absolute being and in limited manifestation.

And I tell you that I have in this Presence tasted more deeply and more intimately of the life or soul of God than of the soul of tree or of flower, of wind or of rain, or of any friend, animal or human; and it is sweet, sweet, ay, sweeter far than any human word can tell.

For the soul knows, in a way that is beyond all doubt, when she does touch the One Life-centre of the great Cosmos. She knows when she feels the touch of, and her contact with the Living God; and nothing, nothing can ever rob her of this knowledge.

And this knowledge satisfies the whole nature, and is the one and only vital food for mind and soul, heart and nerve, flesh and blood.

The name of Jesus.

Surely I can well understand the intense aversion that many of the most spiritual and humane souls have to the very name of Jesus; for I myself was one of them for long time.

For when we think of the many insanities and vagaries of the human religious consciousness that have been intimately associated with the use of this name as of all other such names, we can well see the cause of this aversion.

But its abuse by the unwise does not affect the value of the name in its true power and significance.

For to me the name has come to stand for the whole human sanity of sweetness, gentleness, and all good cheer; manifesting its power in the whole life of a perfect love, whose fruits are ever, and in all circumstances of our most mundane experiences, not only a patient tolerance, but an actual compassion for all creatures, howsoever strange and unseemly be the ways of their self-expression, and howsoever far removed in the beautiful from our own personal tastes and ideals be these experiences.

Thus in the great and one love that loveth every creature, and that can in no way turn itself from any soul, however and whatver be her circumstances, do we find the true significance and content of the very genius of this holy name.

Now "the Church" has made this name utterly ineffective, and even a thing of offence and derision to the world, through her idolatry in trying to fabricate out of a human personality a god.

We do not reproach her for this. She is a human vessel, otherwise she could not do her work, and this human child is ever prone, ay, even after the need to do so has passed, to make unto herself idols.

This has been one of her many errors, as all who know her and love her now admit, but we believe that it has run its great course, and is surely though slowly passing away, for we are assured by the witness within, as well as by many witnesses among our fellows, that the spiritual ear of Christendom is now opening, and in many is already straining eagerly for the true note of the music of the Sun of God, the word of a pure and rational, sweet and sane, simple and utterly whole and self-consistent realization of this one great cosmic and microcosmic, personal and universal fact in the life of the spiritual nature of man, even the great Love of God.

Well knows the taster, the feeler, the knower in our nature, that in this holy Love-presence is the quintessence, consummation, or whole utterance of all the beauty and power, wisdom and sweetness that has been uttered through the great human spiritual consciousness in all the ages of the past, whether the name used has been Ra or Krishna, Hari or Buddha or otherwise for the great and near Love-presence.

Yes, your gentle Buddha, my brother, is in and of the one Christ-spirit, integrally, essentially, inalienably, and is a living word thereof, even as my Jesus is.

It is, even as all these and other unnamed words, an expression of a mode of the great Christ-genius that is unique and all needful for the full utterance of the one holy word of Life and of Love.

And this is why I love to touch with the kiss of my hand the brow even of the image of Buddha or Krishna; and this is why I sign that brow, even as I sign the brow of any soul who is in the service of this great Utterance of God with the sign of the Cross of Life and of Love.

For my Jesus-lover is in the holy Krishna, and my Jesus-peace is in the gentle Buddha, for there is the deep peace, the silent joy, the never passing cheer of the Heart of God, and this is why I can embrace with an all-enfolding love my brother of the East.

☩ ☩ ☩

And so it comes to be that every soul receives, or will receive the holy Thing even as it can receive it. And, inasmuch as what is a food for you now may not be a food for me now, it is only right that we all have an absolute tolerance for the mode of our brother's apprehension of spiritual things. Indeed, indeed, as we all know so well, this is the only possible way of living with one another.

And now when we have given you all that we can give you of our very best, and when we would even have said all that we can say thereon, for it is well on such themes to number our words, does not the one essential fact remain unmoved and unmoveable so far as this utterance is concerned, that here we have in this most personal fellowship a real presence, ay, the real presence of the living God, who is, even as the child in our fathers realised, though dimly and even grotesquely at times, our own Emmanuel, the blessed Jesus-lover, even God come to dwell with us, for us, in us eternally.

Healing through the Power of the Great Beauty, and how this Jesus-Love-Light saves us from our sins.

Now, in this Jesus love-light is the great Beauty of God. Have you ever seen the Eye of the inner light? If so, you will know what I mean when I say that in the Love-light is the power of the great Beauty, for the beauty of the love of the Eye of Life is more than any human word can describe.

Wondrously sweet in its gentle humanity is the wisdom of the Love-light.

For, to the soul it would bless and heal, it shows its beauty little by little, allowing our feeble one to see just as much of this beauty as she can receive at the time, yet ever holding it thus modified or veiled before her opening vision.

This is no phantomal beauty thus held before the vision of the soul. It is a very real, near, and substantial forth-showing of the Divine substance in this most subtle and intimate manifestation of the one holy, ineffable, unnameable Essence.

For be it well noted, as an essential to this word, that in this unveiling and forth-shining a very power of beauty is sent forth and communicated to the aspiring soul, which enables her to follow her quest.

And it abides thus before the vision of the soul, unveiling to her more and more of the great Beauty, even as she becomes more and more able to receive and assimilate the power of the sweet light, thus winning her little by by little, until at last she is won in all her powers and elements, in all her parts and passions, in all her moods and possibilities, in all her inborn human richnesses and prime, virginal simplicities, won, won, won in all these, her present-day hosts and ancient peoples, won through and through to the Life and service of the Beauty of God, ay, so won that these very elements of her once material animal soul are now, through this almighty, transmuting power of Beauty, her own principalities, powers, and glories in her own heavenly places.

And she is now a whole lover, and her body is now a whole body of Love. And she cannot but give of all her strengths and all her virtues to this one Great Lover, and to the service of Love.

And in this yielding of all her virtues, and in this surrender of her whole self-hood in will and desire, she is set free from these olden bonds of the animal self-will which held her during the ages in the bondage of sin and death through their manifold modes of desire.

And in this giving of all her strengths and virtues to the service of the Great Lover is her service of the creature, for she has now the word within her ever saying: If ye would love me, love my body. If ye would serve me well, serve well the most needy and most unloveable of these my members, human and sub-human.

Thus through her love she is at last raised entirely and unalterably into the degree of the whole and absolutely absorbed lover, wherein she cannot sin or fail from satisfying the ideal that now dwells within her.

For she is now all in the Power of the One Beauty, and the Power of the One Beauty is her own power, and there is therefore no power left in her for the sustenance of these ancient uglinesses, and so they pass away, slowly, very slowly it may seem at times, yet surely, until no trace of them remains.

Thus is she delivered from the powers of death; thus is she saved from her sins; thus is she healed of her infirmities and cleansed from her defilements. And this is the Redemption through Love.

And thus, and thus only, is she satisfied.

For it matters not how true and pure the love may be that she receives through a human vessel, she can never be satisfied till she is altogether given unto the beauty of this one love. In fact, all the experiences of the human or limited love are but powers whose very use and purpose is to prepare her as a body for this the one great consummation of her present being.

In all this is the great healing of our whole nature. For, sure as the holy love-light shines through and through the soul, so surely will the whole nature of mind and flesh, of heart and will, be made whole in this beauty.

And this is the coming of the Health of God to our whole nature. And this is the great salvation, or the living and enjoying of the Health of God.

And this health of God cannot but come forth in us, and through and through. For the power of it is ever working within, and it works in the will of Beauty.

And we do not need to be always holding its presence in our conscious mentality in order that the work be done.

For it suffices that it shines and shines within. And it never ceases to shine; for even when your physical or mental consciousness is exhausted, asleep, or otherwise occupied, yet is it shining, ever shining and doing its work. For "they rest not day nor night," for they are the powers of God within you.

Thus the great work of healing is being done, unconsciously oftimes, ay, generally so to the mundane or external consciousness. But the fruits of this silent, continuous work of the holy love-light will appear in good time, and always according to what is best for your health as a slowly evolving spiritual nature, even as it always is in the out-working of the law of Love.

And often you will be utterly astonished at this fruition,

for it comes forth into actual manifestation when you do not look for it and least expect it.

And you can only say: This is surely the doing of the Great Lover, and it is wondrous in our eyes.

For of this there can be no doubt that the high and pure fruition of a fuller and fuller life of body or soul or mind is an ever-increasing power for the enjoying of Life or Beauty or God in all modes of manifestation.

Concerning the Service of the Unveiling of Ugliness.

Now, even as the great service of our health is fulfilled through the unveiling of beauty, so is it through the unveiling of ugliness, whether it be of the personal or the communal soul. Of the former ugliness I have already spoken in the "Song of the Cross," and of the latter in "The Crucifixion and Resurrection of the Soul of Germany."

And even while I write these words is not the hideousness of the present commercial system making itself so manifest, even holding unabashed her most flagrant ugliness before the eyes of all who can see, and saying to all who can hear: Behold me now, me whom you have made your supreme good, behold me the beast of your hell, even me the genius of greed; behold me the one god of your desire in my naked and unashamed ugliness.

Only be it noted that through the service of ugliness there is not, for there cannot be communicated, the power to quit it or deny it as in the service of beauty. For in beauty or love God is, but in greed or ugliness God is not, and there is no power where God is not.

The Great Resurrection.

You know, dear child of Light, the most secret service of the Great Beauty for your cleansing and healing, for has not the Christ in thee, even the all-seeing, all-knowing, all-scrutinizing eye of God within thy nature, looked on and judged all thy quick and thy dead in the resurrection of thy past?

And what a resurrection! All, all, all the past deeds, even of our most secret will, arise before us quick once more in the live light of the one high Beauty of God; and we, yes we our very selves, must pass judgment on them, and through them on this human soul who has been their creator in life.

Well, well for thee, O soul, when thou art allowed so to judge in the light of the Christ-beauty, for then thy judgment is right, condemning the deed but not the doer. For in thy Christ-judgment the great compassion ever covers the frailties even of thine own nature, and we all know how, because of its very sensitiveness to sin, the new thing in us is ever prone to judge of oneself more severely than of the neighbour; and thou art also empowered of Love to deny for ever in thy nature the power, and to rise above these frailties.

But of this be very sure, if there is the torment of self-condemnation it is not the Christ in thee who is judging; but it is the genius of thine own lower nature who is seeking to use thy present feebleness of will for the discomfiture and death of the Holy Lover and Healer who is now, even in this keen resurrection seeking to save thee from her ancient power.

The Genius of the Healer.

The genius of the healer is one with that of the saviour or redeemer.

The healer must save from death, must redeem from sin, and must give his very life in so doing.

And in order to save from sin, or to heal a soul or a body, he is, as a healer, ready, ever ready to give all he has; for he is in the will of the one Giver who gives all.

Not blindly nor in the power of a passing impulse does he act.

For he knows the whole situation and the demands thereof, and he virtually says: I am ready. I shall not seek to save my life. I shall withold nothing. I shall not seek in any way to avoid this negative condition. I know its nothingness in the one Essence. I can meet and overcome it.

For, if this power of the living Christ, or the one great Love, is really alive in him, he is able to meet and overcome all conditions, how trying soever they may be to his human nature, even as the power of the sun meets and overcomes the miasmas and mists of earth.

And this realisation of the invincible and all-conquering power is the one thing that then really matters; for it is the very panoply of Spirit, and the soul who is clothed in it cannot be hurt by any adverse force.

✠ ✠ ✠

Now there are no relationships in life in which this will not prove itself so.

It has been my privilege, I say so most seriously, to be allowed to help not a few of these heroes of the good, the true, and the beautiful Thing of our day and of our land, who have not hesitated to suffer all hardships rather than violate the holy law of their nature which says: "Thou shalt not kill thy brother."

For, when they have asked me what their attitude towards their judges should be, I have spoken thus:—

When you are about to face the tribunal, go unto these men as to your own brothers, and in the spirit of service, saying thus in your heart:—

"I believe I possess something of good that these men do not possess, and I will to give to them any of this good that I can give. This I shall do in the power of holy Love."

And to their judges I have asked them thus to say, if allowed:—

"I do understand and sympathise with you in your desire to fulfil what you feel to be your duty. I believe you are animated with the desire to do the right. I believe you are sincere.

And I only ask you to credit me now with the same desire and the same sincerity of heart."

The words are, and should be few, even as all words of power are few.

But I can say that the results of this course have been such as have over and over again astonished even me the suggestor.

Assuredly it has placed these men in the place of true power and their judges have felt it so, and have regarded these men, according to their confession, as their judges.

And it has certainly allowed the powers of the invisible world to work for their deliverance.

The stories I could tell you of the ways in which even the shrewdest and keenest army doctors have been made, yes, actually made to work for their deliverance, are such as I could hardly ask you to credit. Yet are these as truly matters of fact as that I am now addressing you.

Verily the hand of God still worketh wondrously for the deliverance of the pure and innocent from the hands of the ruthless violator of the most gentle beauty of life. And blessed indeed are they who are able to put all their trust therein.

Concerning the Keeping of Times for Healing.

Now this work, if it is done at all, is fulfilled in the spirit where there is neither a time nor a space condition, nor any other limitation of the outer realm of manifestation.

Therefore it is altogether unnecessary, and a useless task to trouble about times for doing the work.

And this is self evident to the worker, who knows that it would become an absolute impossibility in the very nature of things to keep in mind such temporal and other considerations if he would really do the work.

And we know well, and say now as plainly as our words can, that it suffices that you, ay, even you, human soul, say to thy Holy One within, who never slumbers nor sleeps: I will thee to be present to such and such a soul in the power of thy healing virtue. And this your will of good shall be done, for it is the will of God.

✠ ✠ ✠

When the power thus to send forth thy Holy One comes to thee, O sonl, there is no refreshing or recreating influence, whether it be of sun, or air, or scene, whether of a purely physical or psychic, mental or spiritual beauty and good, that you may not send to the soul, whether incarnate or decarnate, whom you would serve in Life.

Is it needful for me to say again that in this place of service incarnate and decarnate are indeed one?

But of this I shall now speak more fully.

Many are the degrees of Sensitiveness.

Only the soul who has vowed herself to the service of the great suffering Soul of our creation knows what suffering is.

And to those fine sensitives of the Soul of the suffering Christ I would give as a word of comfort what I have often had to give for the comfort of those gentle lovers of the lower animals, who make the mistake of attributing to these lowly creatures the sensitiveness that pertains in nature to their own finer quality, and to it alone.

For Nature is greatly merciful, and of a truth these

creatures do not, for they cannot, suffer as we do, for from the plant to the animal there are many and varying degrees of sensitiveness.

And so it is with the finely sensitive servant of Love who feels so keenly, and makes the mistake of crediting that same power of suffering to the soul he would serve, when that soul is, in very fact, not yet capable of such feeling.

Yes, and we repeat it: holy nature is greatly merciful. She is indeed the manifestor and the forthgiver of the goodness of God.

The Great Sacrifice to Love.

The great sacrifice, typified in the slaying of beasts according to the Mosaic and kindred rituals that every soul who truly aspires unto the service of the Best or Highest has to make unto this one Good Thing, is the sacrifice, first, of all the desires and propensities of the lower nature, such as greeds, jealousies, hates, petty meannesses, and the unnamed unworthinesses and falsities of all kinds which come to us out of the present, and which we have brought with us out of our past, either of this life or of other lives; and then finally and utterly, of the will of the old-time self who cannot but seek to dominate or have its own way with the will of the other.

These hereditary or native propensities constitute the beast in us, and our work as free-born spirits is, soon as we realise that we are free-born in will, deliberately and persistently to sacrifice them all to this Good Thing in us.

This work is done, first by denying their power in us and then by refusing them all satisfaction or sustenance in or through our nature.

Thus are they gradually extirpated root and branch; for in denying them a place in the activities of our nature we cut at the root, and in refusing to them any satisfaction we starve them bodily.

It is in the fulfilling of this great work of the will of God that we enter consciously and effectively into the service of the cosmic Lamb whose life is given for the bearing away of the sins of the world, and who is therefore, for the human soul, the best or highest in service to which she may aspire.

For, in thus deliberately sacrificing the lower nature in our own flesh and heart and soul, we work through the co-operation of all our good in will and desire with the great aspiring soul of the one Good in humanity, and we thus fulfil the great eucharistic sacrifice, not for our own good only but for the good of all.

Surely my brother, surely my sister, in this most holy service of Life, you can see that in thus doing and ever doing, you are actually, and in the reality of very deed, giving, ever giving your flesh and your blood for the salvation or health of the whole world, and that through you, yes, even through your humanity is being fulfilled the perpetual and age-long self-sacrifice of the great Love.

The only way of Peace.

Peace comes neither by the death of the body nor of any of the powers of the body. This we all know well.

Peace, the great Peace, the Peace of God, the only Peace, comes through the death of the powers of the old self-nature by their passing away into the power of the new man. Rivalries, jealousies, contentious strivings, hates and all modes of warring between brothers or sisters or any men or women cease only when the powers of this old animal nature, which manifest in her self-pride, self-will and all manner of selfishnesses are renounced or are yielded and given over utterly as a whole sacrifice to the Holy One of the soul, even the great Love.

And, even as this is so in you and in me, so is it in the soul of these peoples of this earth.

And no peace can come to our labouring world nor to her weary children until they too have renounced the old self with all her prides.

Now, among brothers or sisters or any men or women it is always the maturer, the stronger, the wiser ones who lead in the way of peace.

Long time since their motto in life has been: Rather would I die than do the selfish deed.

They know what are the essential and all-needful conditions of peace, and they are now strong enough in the true spiritual nature to do these things, *i.e.* to fulfil the law of the great Love.

They know that the holy Love covers all the past and wipes out all sense of wrong received.

They know that, so long as even the thought of any wrong received abides alive in the heart, the true Love is not yet made perfect in them.

They know this so well; and because they are indeed wise in the knowledge of the values of life, they have seen to it that they shall, even in this, be holy, *i.e.* perfect as a vessel of Love.

And so, just for the sake of Love, (and that always is for the sake of these others,) they sanctify their whole nature, they renounce all the rights of this old self-hood, and they lay all her prides and desires beneath the feet even of the very lowliest of their kind.

They know so well that all these ideas of the rights and prides of the lower self are, in the light of the true wisdom of life, of the nature of delusions and even of insanities; and, once and for all, they deny the power of these unrealities in their heart.

And because we still feel, yea know, with the sure knowledge of the soul, that this great Anglo-Celtic-Saxon race, represented in America and in all these lands beyond the seas as truly as in these our islands, is the stronger in Love and the wiser in the knowledge of life, or, if you prefer it, the least selfish of all these others, we call on her now to lay all her self-prides, with their manifold hypocrisies and other falsities and her sense of self-rights, on the altar of the great human weal, so that she may not fail at this time to make full use of this supreme opportunity to rise to her high calling in God, and so fulfil her great destiny as the servant of Love among men.

We know this to be her high calling in Life; and we shall continue to affirm that she cannot allow any of these false eidola, these delusions of the old self-hood, to prevent her from becoming in actual fact what she is in the will of heaven, but that she shall realise her destiny and do, even in these days, her bit, her own God-given bit, for the health of the soul of this world as the servant of Love to these others.

And if only she is thus able to do this good thing, she will soon find that these others will unite, ay even France with Germany, in vieing with one another to follow her lead in the way of the blessed Life.

✠ ✠ ✠

But we know that she shall be won, yea is, in the true realm of her being, already won for the Christ-ideal and the high calling or service thereof. And all we who see and affirm this are doing the best that we can do towards its realisation.

Now, before the final triumph of the great Love in the soul there is, of necessity and without fail, the supreme struggle for existence on the part of these old-time powers.

It is their fight to the death, for they feel that the time of their extinction is at hand. And the manifestations of this struggle are usually such as baffle the power of the ordinary human understanding.

And so we may in these days look for this supreme struggle in the soul of this great race.

And we may therefore expect very strange, bewildering, and, to the ordinary mundane sense of right, it may be even appalling manifestations through the death-agony of these old-time powers, as well as all manner of the subtle subterfuges, pretentions, and other crafty devices for a continued existence on the part of this old selfhood ere it passes away from our race.

But, inasmuch as we know that these untoward manifestations most surely portend the end of the old regime, we can well afford to look on even the most appalling of them in the calm assurance of the soul who knows that this agony is but the harbinger of the triumph of the holy Thing, and that these strange happenings are but the symptoms of the forthcoming of a finer, higher, sweeter and more abundant life than heretofore known to our earth.

And if indeed, to rise to and utter the ultimate of what we see to be possible, the time of the great fruit-bearing has come for the spiritual soul or Christ-kernel of this great race, and this holy seed of her great body is found of the Trier and Knower of all to be ready to be sown by the winds of Life unto the ends of the earth, could those who love her well, and who know that the supreme good of the mature is even thus to be sown broadcast for the quickening, enriching and beautifying of the waste places, deny to her the joy, or retard her, even if this were possible to the power of the love of their personal will, from entering into the blessedness, of the giver of all the good she can give unto these younger children of the One Mother.

For the maturer soul must give, ever give, and the younger must eat, ever eat.

Such is the law of life, and we do not well when we deny or violate this law either in our personal, or social, our national or international relationships.

But the will of Life shall be done, for it alone is in the one only Being, and there is no hand that can turn it aside.

And so we can say to all even now in fullest confidence: It is well, it is well, and again it is well.

And to the gentle and timorous ones we can say: Good cheer, good cheer, and again good cheer. Possess your soul in the great Peace, for your deliverance is nearer than you can realise. Behold the day of the new humanity is dawning; and it is well, it is well, and again it is well.*

The Love-Bath.

I am sure that many of you know what I mean by the Love-bath, for is it not almost a daily or hourly need of your heaven-born nature?

In the service of the great compassion the healing body of your nature has taken into it some of the breath of the virus, which is the poison of death in the soul you have sought to serve, and the withdrawing of which from this soul has been the work of your present compassion.

---

* How often during these days of this truly wonderful *denouement* in the surrender of the powers of force to what is unquestionably a world-combine towards a better regime have I been asked by the children of the dawn if all this did not mean that the millenial peace was upon us; and I have had once more to say, however it may have hurt the optimism of these children: "No, no, no; for until Love reigns there shall be, for there can be, no peace."

In our own nature, in our homes and in all our relationships we know that Love alone can bring forth the Holy Thing, the Child of Peace, and so long as greed and hate are among us there must be war; and greed and hate and vain-glorying and pride in the power of our Armada are still in us; and where they are there the great peace cannot be.

A police-peace, a peace of force? Yes, that is possible and more than likely, and we are thankful even for this one fruit of our labour; for that it is even possible is a sure sign of the onward trend of the human cause, for it was not possible a century ago.

And so to all our Jeremiahs we must affirm with Galileo, "*Pure se muove.*" Yes, she moves, she moves, she moves. Our world-genius moves ever onward and upward. And for this we thank God.

For, when the personal sympathies are very intense, we can so easily become tainted with the physical, psychic or mental poisons which we, as healers, naturally draw forth through the virtue of our healing qualifications from those whom we greatly desire to serve in love, or, we may actually be defiled by merely coming into contact with their uncleanness of thought, or of feeling, or of physique.

It may be that the disorder manifests as an unnamed misery, or an undefined woe, or it may be as a certain hate or a well-defined grudge, a feeling of wrong or resentment, either justified in its own sphere and right according to its own law, or altogether imagined and false.

Whatever be the expression or mode matters not.

You know too well that in entering into that soul's state you have been tainted in your finer body by the breath of its malady.

Now this poison-taint would work its own work of death in your whole nature were you to allow it to bide with you.

So you must betake you at once, and as for very dear life's sake, to the waters of cleansing.

In fact, the healer in whom this holy Thing works freely and fully will be constrained to seek these waters, and as soon as possible.

Now, how best is the bath taken, and how best made effective?

By beginning, if need be, even by the help of a conscious self-will, to pour forth blessing, calling it forth into actual power by the use of such a word as "God bless every soul," and by continuing to utter this will of blessing, persistently it may even be, until you feel that you are clean through and through.

It is well when such a service may be fulfilled amid the strong and sweet airs and clean surroundings of some wind-swept, sun-kissed spot, such as the lonely sea-shore, or the fresh, grassy hillside, for there the powers of holy nature will work with the powers of the Holy Genius of our health.

There yield you to, and so allow these willing servants of God's health to work with your own Holy One of healing the sweet work of washing clean, restoring and renewing your whole nature, even she who is indeed the fine vessel of God, so precious, so precious for the sake of the service as to be cared for with all the wisdom of life at your disposal.

This is a very pleasant and altogether beautiful way of Love's washing.

Sometimes the modes are neither so pleasant to feel nor so beautiful to see, but howsoever they appear, blessed, blessed, ever blessed is the work of the waters of the Great Love of God.*

✠ ✠ ✠

There is another mode of the service of the bath of Love which is even more beautiful in its action than this, for it is through the service of the finest, sweetest, purest soul that our humanity has yet produced.

I know well of what I speak here, for I have been

---

* Out of the above will arise a much-needed light on the great doctrine of Karma as so often taught and received in these days.

For I have found not a few most gentle, sweet, and righteous souls who have long time been held in torment or in deep despair through the belief that they and they alone can and must work out their Karmic debt.

Now we have all to pay our whole debt to the law and we shall not leave our prison till it is all paid.

But, but, and here is just the needed word of light, the soul who has come into the full power and service of the great Love can give to the feeble one of her power to do, to the debtor of her abundant, ay, inexhaustible riches wherewith to pay.

And if that soul can and will only receive this as the free gift of Love, not only will her deliverance from the bonds of Karma and the hell of guilt be hastened but she will pass to the degree where this law is transcended by the higher law of Love.

This we know to be one of the great human services of Life. And we know it through abundant experiences.

privileged to meet not a few of these choice vessels of the Great Love who in them actually takes unto its very bosom not only the sore conditions but even the elements, physical and psychic of the world-soul, using them and consuming them in its own nature for their transmutation; and I have been allowed to witness for years and to study the nature of this most holy power in the gentle person of the little one whom the Christ-mother so graciously gave me to care for in her name.

Concerning this most hidden and most beautiful of Life-services I would fain speak to you, but suffice it to say now that I know those who have passed through all the most painful and trying experiences of the men at the front, even unto the bearing in their own sweet soul and sinless flesh the loathesomeness of the moral leprosies that ever crawl about and lie in wait to capture and destroy these men; or in actually being blown to pieces in the astral body or the bringing back in their very flesh from the front the marks of wounds which have been certified by the best of physicians as bullet wounds; but even to you my reader it is well not to talk much of these matters here.

And when, in their human revolt against such a moral affliction, they have asked me why it is that they were called on so to suffer, I could only reply: " Because you are found worthy. By the very action of the great selfless Love in your will you have asked to be allowed to bear these loathesomenesses and to consume and so annul the power of these sins and of their death; and your prayer has only been answered."

The Way of the Great Peace.

When the soul comes to this God-consciousness in which it sees the hand of Love aworking in all things it enters into rest from all its labouring.

It not only ceases from all common anxiety or care,

but it ceases even to feel that it must be ever fighting the good fight.

For it knows now that it needs not to fight, but only to let God work.

It ceases from all strenuous effort of self-will even in the cause of any good.

For it knows that this too is God's affair, and that, if only it allows God to work through it, the most effective of all propaganda or other services of life shall be effected through it.

And, as a sure result, it will cease from rousing the antagonism of the dark or retrogressive powers whether in the seen or the unseen realms of our existence.

It will not have to drink the martyr's cup in the usual sense of this expression, for it has willingly crucified self, and given its very soul unto the hands of the good services of the adversary, tormentor and slayer of the self-will.

And now the old self-will is no more, and there are no elements in its body of effectivity that need the fiery service of the crucible of Life.

In the Wilderness.

How often have I sat before this picture of Elijah * in the wilderness in the Liverpool Art Gallery, certainly not attracted to it by any distinct artistic power, for that I do not find in it, but because it shows to me, in a very simple and vivid light, this my actual, present experience. The angel — the conventional, well-fleshed figure with wings, only they are not even white, they are of gaudy colours, exactly like those of certain parrots!—stands by the exhausted figure of Elijah, who is sound asleep, and he looks down on it with a certain pitying curiosity, as much as to say: "What a strange, wild creature this is whom I am sent to feed—half-animal, half-man; certainly more animal than divine!"

* By Leighton.

Yes, here I have more than once during these later years shed the tears of the love of a grateful heart, for I have seen in that weary figure this human personality utterly worn out with the sore labours of these years, and in this angel I have seen a picture of my own Holy One, my Mother and my Father, my Lover and my Friend, even this hidden Jesus of the heart, who has come out of the great Deep of Love to stand by this weary soul through these long nights and days in the wilderness, wherein so often I have not been able to see one green spot, or to taste one drop of living water, and when the only word left to me was:—Thou alone, O Jesu-Love, thou alone, art able to keep me through it all.

How the Great Patience comes to us and Saves us from Error.

When we look back through our experiences in life, is it not very clear to us that the great work ever wrought-out, in and through them all, has been the bringing of the wild, crude elements of our nature into a finer order of life?

I doubt not that the wild plant or fruit-tree suffers in its own way through the process of culture. In like manner these crude, harsh elements of our savage or uncultivated nature do not wish to give up their present existence. But their primeval strengths are needed in the service of Life; and they must be won.

Hence the process; hence the fight; hence the pain. For the great work must be done. It is the will of Life; and there is no power that can keep these elements from being ultimately gathered into the greater beauty of Life.

And surely, when through close and near study, we get even a little glimpse of the manifold process of the great work of the redemption of all these elements of our nature, and realize even ever so feebly how very gradual and, to our seeing, how very, very slow, this work must be, we will also realize to this same degree how very patient we must be, first toward ourselves, for to my finding that is the more difficult, and then towards one another, *i.e.* towards every soul.

For the great redemption is not complete until all these elements of our nature that we have drawn unto us and made our belongings throughout all the experiences of all our past lives or states of existence, have been cleaned, sweetened, transmuted in quality and absorbed into the new body and soul of the great Love-light.

Thus, as an example and to illustrate this point as briefly as I can:

We are all so familiar, either in ourselves or in others, with the reproach that we do not practise what we preach, or that we do not manifest in our own life what we profess in doctrine; and the term hypocrite is freely used accordingly.

Now sometimes it is rightly so used, but not always, and, I feel, not generally, through misunderstanding.

For we know that in the order of this great work of redemption the vision of life always must come long before the whole and complete realization. And indeed this is so through all modes of our nature's unfoldment in life.

There is the seeing, then the desire and the long process of realizing, and then the apprehension and assimilation.

And so here. First, a very, very faint glimmer of light, and we simply know that we see something that we had never seen before. Gradually as the eye becomes stronger this light increases until a great vision of beauty dawns on the soul, and she must declare her vision and sing her song of this, to her, the whole Beauty of God. And she does sing her song, and her singing is acceptable and a good to the human soul.

But she has not yet been able to take unto herself but

a very little of the power or essence of the vision, partial even though it must be, because of limitations; and the result is that there are many shortcomings, apparent relapses, and frequent inconsistencies. And when we see this we are usually impatient and often blaspheme our own soul or the soul of the brother.

Now the fact of nature is that it will take a long period, probably more than one lifetime, for this soul to assimilate all the power of the Beauty that she has seen even in this limited vision of God.

For she is in the process of becoming, and ever becoming; and though appearances would seem to justify the old reproach that she is " ever learning and never arriving," we know that she is coming ever nearer and nearer unto the one sure consummation of the great work of God in her nature, even her unification in all her powers, through her assimilation of all the Beauty, and her utter oneness in and with the great Blessedness of Life. And a great and sweet patience begins to come to us, and in time it too becomes our very own.

Now this patience is in the sweet wisdom of Christ, for it is the fruit of a true vision, apprehension and knowledge of the process of our nature's unfolding, from the time when she receives the first ray of light even unto her whole absorption into the power of the Beauty of God.

And, being the fruit of true wisdom, it is in the very health of God, and saves us from forming wrong or imperfect judgments concerning the destiny and final state of ourselves and others, and from the nameless despair which this false conception of the great trend and sure issue of the work of God in man certainly brings as its baleful fruit to so many of the lovers of their kind.

Indeed it saves us from all manner of despairings concerning ourselves and others,—the loss of hope, for example, which indeed, in our limited, personal soul, is not to be wondered at, when to all appearances the soil which we have laboured so long still yields the rank, coarse growths of the old selfhood instead of the finely fragrant and beautiful fruits of the blessed Spirit.

Truly wonderful in its perfection is this work of the Great Redemption, for there is no hurtful power of will or of tormenting thought in our whole experience as men and women that it cannot save us from.

Thus how often, and for how long, have you and I tortured ourselves in self-condemnation by regrets for some apparently foolish cause of action in our past career; and we may not even be charitable enough to allow that what we did was done for the best, so far at least as we could see the best at the time.

Well now, let us once and for all set free the weary soul from this most cruel state of self-torment by declaring in the name of Love that there are no experiences in our past life, wherein we may have "missed the mark" of success, and so sinned from our course in due order, none, no none, how painful soever they may have been, either in their then or after fruition, and how disastrous soever to our worldly-wise appreciation of values may have been their effects in our "career," in which our Holy One has not been, and through which our Holy One has not well served the greater good of our true nature, and the fuller health of our true selfhood.

Now, dear soul, this is verily the truth of God, and the whole of it is truth; and if you only get a good hold of it, and realize its virtue, it will certainly save you from the untold torments of regret, and the bottomless hell of remorse, for you will be able now to point to that long past experience and say: There, even there, shone the holy Love-light. There, even there, I see my Saviour.

For, on careful analysis, they will all be found, ay, every one of these effects, to have been the most potent workers in the great process of the disintegration of the self-preservative principle of your old nature, which principle, above all others, must be utterly dissolved and taken away before you, human soul, can enter into the fulness of the blessed life.

But be it noted in passing, the aforesaid is only the other side of the great positive fact that there is no service howsoever lowly, or even to appearance, trifling, into which our home or other duties call us to go, that this Holy One will not enter with us, and not only enable us to fulfil, but will out of the fulfilment win for us a new beauty and a fresh strength, and a sweeter and fuller life.

For in very truth be it reaffirmed to you, the feeble, trembling little child, for your healing: Love, the great Economist, uses all the labours of all our nature in this work of transmutation and redemption, ay, though it appears to be a toil utterly fruitless of good and the most thankless of tasks. Thus, ye gentle, human souls, who through no fault of your own, but simply through circumstances into which ye apparently had, *nolens volens*, to enter, have to pass your days and years in the most cruel and most hard, because most unsatisfying order and form of labour of body, or of soul, or of mind.

Think ye that this your sore labour of sheer ennui is lost, or is utterly of no avail for any good?

Ah, you do think so; and who would expect you to feel otherwise? And this thought is the very torment of hell to your sensitive and conscientious nature.

But my Saviour-Christ assures you that it is not all loss, and that you can even take all these nameless agonies of your soul and your mind and your body, and offer them them to the service of the Master-hand in this the great work of the transmutation and redemption of the powers of the soul of our race.

Yes, it is indeed a sure, it is a sane, it is a good thing, this great patience of Christ in our nature, for it is founded on the apprehension of the one great and holy principle of our being which knows that God is in the world, that the all-knowing, all-pervading, all-fathering, all-mothering One is essentially and eternally in the minutest as well as in the greatest manifestations of Life, and that therefore all, all is well with our world-soul, with your soul, my fellow-pilgrim in Life, and with even my soul.*

How we who are in this Power can, and do serve the World-Soul.

We are now actually in the power of this Holy Love, and we cannot but do the work thereof.

We are now generators and forth-givers of the potency of the Christ-seed, and we are thus energizers of the world-soul.

In this, our very own and rightful work, we are only doing for her what was done for our psyche through the manifold and holy services of the Great Lover in all those who have been, throughout all our lives, our nourishing fathers and our nourishing mothers in God.

And we shall continue to do this work of her blessing; ever, ever giving to her need of the very best of our strength, until her own Christ has been formed in her, and her own Sun has come forth into actual existent potency as her saviour-healer and her leader into her own whole blessedness. Nor shall we cease from this work, whether it be in the super-conscious, conscious, or sub-conscious degrees of our being, until her redemption is complete, and her health is made perfect.

✠ ✠ ✠

Why is it that the soul strives for nothing so much as to be delivered from the power of the personal affections in the love-relationship?

* The great labour of the human genius towards the better exists because of the inertia latent in the very elements through and in which she has to labour and herein is a sure light on the reasonableness of the great patience.

Why is she never satisfied nor at rest till she has become a giver rather than a seeker after love?

It is that so long as we desire to receive the good of the love of any other soul we are held in bond to that soul, being her debtor just in the degree to which we have sought after and received of her love.

And we shall not be set free from this bondage till we have paid this debt " unto the uttermost farthing."

The Great Service of the Temple.

Now, once you have made the utter and absolute offering of your whole nature, just as you are, this being the whole oblation of your love, you are accepted by Love even as you are.

And you become then and therein, and in virtue of this one act of your whole will, a worker in the holy service of Life; and you are received into the great service of the temple of Health, and you are robed according to the degree of your spiritual unfoldment by the Hand of power in the fair robe of a higher consciousness,—a robe that, inasmuch as it is the Christ-consciousness in you, becomes fairer and finer, stronger and more enduring, as the genius of your growth in these degrees demands and provides.

And you, human soul, are now a king and a priest unto God for ever, anointed with the oil of an eternal blessedness, and crowned with the unfailing power of the Christly peace, wherein is the very wellspring of the joy that passeth never away.

Yes, I say, you human soul, whosover you be and how lowly soever you stand either in the esteem of your fellows or of yourself.

And in truth, and as a very fact, the more and more fit you become for this robe of Life, the simpler and simpler will become your ways of life and thought, and the sweeter and lowlier your estimate of yourself, and the keener and finer your sensitiveness to aught in your nature that is not altogether in the great Beauty.

And now that you are initiated into the great service of the Temple of Life, you never can cease from the service, nor go forth from the holy place of your power.

For here are temples within temples, even unto the deep, deep infinity of the Innermost.

And you pass from the outer to enter the inner.

And so it is through all your lives unto the ages of ages for you, O human soul, sweet vessel of life, through whom the joy of God has once, ay, even once flowed.

For soon as you are fit, *i.e.*, as soon as your new robe is ready, you enter the new temple to fulfil the services thereof.

This passing from one degree into another is fulfilled in this body just as it is fulfilled in the super-physical planes of our existence.

And so it is, that even in this body you can never cease from this most holy service, for in whatever work you be engaged, how mundane soever it be, and even though it appear to be no work, *e.g.*, merely listening to a soul pouring forth its story to you, you are ever, ever in the actual service of the will of blessing.

For you cannot but bless; and even while this little one is unburdening itself to you, the whole nature is opening herself, and is thus receiving the blessing of Life through you.

And thus it is, as we have so often said, and I do love to repeat it: during night and day, in sleeping and in awaking, in the hours of our most conscious activity in the external work of life, even as in the hours of our most intense silence, whether we be in the body or out of it, and wheresoever we be, and in whatever state of mental or psychic consciousness we may be, we are in the Great Work, and the work is fulfilling itself in and through us; and we cease not day nor night to sing with those who ever sing the ageless Song of Life: Holy, Holy, Holy, O Great Love art Thou, the universe is full of thy glory, the whole creation breathes thy sweetness and sings forth thy beauty.

And this holy service of the one Temple is thy destiny, O reader of this word, whosoever thou art.

And thou shalt assuredly come to it in good time.

O wondrous is the Beauty of Life, and wondrous the service thereof.

And for this Beauty, and for her service, thou art.

A Service we can all render in all circumstances at all times to all people and to all creatures.

It matters not who the soul is, it matters not what its past or present life may be, it matters not what anybody tells you about this one, you can always bless this soul, yes, even this soul, here and now.

It matters not though you have never seen this one before and know nothing whatsoever about this personality, you can now give unto it the silent blessing of love.

And be assured, that it is indeed blessed in your blessing, and the more effectively so, in that the blessing is given from the super-personal degree of our spiritual nature.

Jesus plays in the Smile of Blessing.

This morning, I said to my old friend, "Jack," the bus conductor, "It always does me good to see you, Jack. You have done good to thousands without knowing anything of it, and that simply by the playful light of your eye and the health of your smile."

The dear fellow was indeed surprised to be told that he had been thus uttering the word of God through all these long years of a comparatively grimy and aimless toil on the board of a London bus.

But he had the spiritual acumen to perceive the truth of what I said, and that is why I could say it; and now he knows that he is indeed, even in the good cheer of his smile and the play of his fun, serving God well in thus serving the life of his fellows.

Marvellous indeed is the truth hidden herein. For the Holy Child plays, and plays, and ever plays, and in and through its simple play there is communicated the very finest power of health.

I could tell of some wondrous proofs I've had of this lately. But for these days words must be few. The facts are here, and they suffice.

Healing through the Written Word.

I know that there is healing in the written word for many have declared this to me concerning my own writings.

Words are things of reality. They are the strength of your whole nature, and your very life-blood is in them.

For a true word is alive, and it is no word if it is not alive.

And thought-entities or powers dwell in these words, and they are in being or essence according to the quality of these words.

And they work out the will of their own genius, whether it be for life or for death, for health or for disease.

Thus it is that any uttered word of blessing will always contain the power of blessing, and this power will always be found therein by the soul who seeks in truth and love to find it.

The Utter Simplicity of the Great Service.

When we realise how utterly simple and natural are the ways of the great service of Life, so much so that we often fail to realise it in fact, we find that there is not any mode of the expression of our most ordinary life that has not in it the possibility of a true service, and may not be used accordingly.

The very common delusion that we must do or feel something out of the usual, so very often holds our powers of blessing within its paralysing bonds, while the fact is that in the forth-uttering of what may be to our mundane valuation the merest triviality—it may be a little song, it may be a friendly visit, it may be a little word of cheer or of sympathy or even a smile—is the very word of life to this soul, and gives to it just what it needs for its enlivening or healing.

Oh, let us be children, ever playing the holy play of innocence in whatsoever circumstances we may be, and however we may feel. Let us just be the little child, and assuredly it will bless this other now

Thus are we in the divine carelessness of what is to be, doing the little deed ever, and ever doing the deed, and leaving it there with God.

Thus are we in the true place of power even with and in the One will of Life. And of a truth all our experience has made it clear to us that when there is no thought whatsoever of fruitage the fruitage is best. For it is whole being of the union of living and doing.

✠ ✠ ✠

Hav'nt children funny little ways of saying and doing things? They love to see us in the beauty of normality, in the simplicity of our holy human nature.

Yestre'en I was walking with four of my Liverpool bairnies in the field of Kelmscott.

The sun was setting in great glory and I was watching it as we walked. Then as he was sinking I began to talk to him, when I found that several little hands were laid on my mouth and were kept there.

It reminded me of the great aversion we children had to hear our father wax so vehement as to become rapt under the power of inspiration when speaking publicly.

Now there is a reason for this in the child-nature, and I leave you to find the reason. I think I've got it in the above heading, for they know and love the Beauty of God.

Liberation for Service.

Wondrous, wondrous is the working of the Hand that would liberate its servant for the service of the Great Love.

We may be sure that the process, even as these other liberating processes, shall not be without pain to the old, self-loving nature.

But we may also be sure that it will not cease till it has fulfilled its blessed will for you, even your utter deliverance from all the cares and impedimenta that would prevent you from entering fully into the joyous life of the greater service.

And these pains of unbinding, and these birth-throes that you wept over, you will now love, esteem and sing of as the very servants of God in your life, and thus even now you may sing:

O my soul, when thou hast fulfilled to the uttermost all the services of this human home, forth thou shalt fare on the wings of the morning, free, free, free to go wheresoever the greater service of good calls thee.

Thus the great work is done, as naturally, spontaneously, unconsciously or unknowingly as are fulfilled all the great services of the blessed powers of the life of our nature.

As freely and as unknowingly does the healer thus heal or bless through his presence or word or thought as do the sun and the birds, the winds and the flowers, the rains and the frosts, and all the holy forces of nature, bless and ever minister unto the soul of every living creature.

And you thus become a living centre, a very near and live body of blessing that ever fulfils the services of Life, *e.g.* in fructifying or enriching and sweetening the social and even the physical atmosphere of our cosmos.

And, wherever you live or pass or breathe amid our human kind, you breathe forth the Holy Thing of Life, and it vitalises, and it cleanses, and it prepares the breath of the world for the nourishing and the supporting of the finer life that is to be, even the life of the Child of the new Day.

The Health of God.

This is the health of the whole nature, of "body, soul and mind," and of all that these terms connote.

And assuredly, human soul, whosoever you be, the will of Life is that you be in the full enjoyment of Life in all the modes and degrees of your existence and in all the bodies, powers or faculties thereof. Surely this is clear enough.

God wills not disease or disorder of any kind. But when through the violation of the Holy Law either on our part or on that of our ancestors, and whether wrought in ignorance or in wilfulness, it is called into existence, it must according to the nature of our cosmos, manifest in the fruition of ill.

And God can and does use it for the greater good of your deathless nature.

For, even as we have said so often: There is no power nor force, how negative soever it be, that Love cannot use in the great service of our fuller blessedness.

"For Christ's Sake."

Does not a new interpretation and appreciation of this holy word of our childhood's prayer arise naturally and come forth spontaneously, as doth all true fruition, out of this finding by the soul of her most vital intimacy with the holy Lover?

For when she realises that there is no word of our

human, affectional intimacy, whether it be as father or mother or sister or brother or lover or friend, that may not in all truth be applied to the facts of this most holy relationship, she will find that she must, in the honour of love, do all she can for the expressing in her life of the will of this holy One who wills, and ever works in her for the fulfilling of her whole good.

Yes, she will say, and this word once wholly uttered in her, will never cease to utter itself in her life: For thy sake, even for thine own sake, my Friend, my Lover, and because thou hast thus given thyself to me, I shall sanctify my whole nature. For thy sake, O Servant of my blessedness, I shall serve thee well in me. And thou shalt see of the fruit of the travail of thy Love in my life, and thou shalt be satisfied.*

Concerning the Service in Healing of the Risen Body of our Humanity.

We know that the less and less gross our whole nature becomes in the physical, psychic, and other degrees of her being, the finer and finer and more potent is the power that can work in and through her.

* Surely this is the very pith of the great fact in our nature, that we can, if so we will and are able, make ourselves partakers in the sufferings of the Christ of the ages of our race.

For the more deeply I see into this relationship the more do I feel that in this Holy One, the Angel of the human good, there is all that must correspond to that in us which can suffer and to the actual suffering itself, only, be it noted, in an infinitely exalted degree and therefore in ways of which we can now only form a very, very feeble conception. And in this bed-rock truth of our nature is found the *raison d'être* for the desire of the soul when she is uttering her highest will to be altogether in the suffering of the Great Lover of our world. For thus indeed she can make of her suffering part of the Great Suffering, and become a sharer of and a fellow-worker in the age-long labour of the redeeming Love. And thus will she not only deliver herself from all the fret or woe of suffering but will receive it gladly as the gift of love, and make of it a priceless power of blessing.

This is a well-established fact of first importance running through all nature.

In the most humdrum experiences of life we have observed that just as the physical vessel becomes finer and finer, or, if you will, more delicate in texture, the more and more immune it becomes to the common ailments, such, *e.g.*, as colds, than the more fleshy and sturdier types.

Does it not therefore follow in reason that they whom we call " the unseen company of the ascended," the great white brotherhood of healers who now dwell in the super-physical, and form in our decarnate humanity the risen body of the Lord of our Life, are vessels of a finer and more potent power of Life than are we who are yet clothed in flesh ?

And that this is verily so is the reason why any doctrine of the great healing Genius of our race that does not give to this fine body of mediatorial service its place and its due in the holy economy of the great Body of the Lord of our Life, is not a whole doctrine or a complete word of the being of our humanity.

Concerning the Infection of the Healer by Negative Conditions.

I have been often asked by healers how they should act in order not to take on the diseased conditions, physical, psychic, or otherwise of their patients, and I have found it right to suggest that they should, as soon as they have left their patient, speak the word of power to these conditions, denying their reality in being, and declaring that they have no power in themselves.

For it is a fact that many of the most sympathetic healers are so affected even unto the serious disorder and disolution of their physique, and it is not right that it should be so.

And this is in no way a denying of the great truth in our human nature, that the sacrifice of self for others is always beautiful in itself, and so much so that the highest honour is paid to the healer in the cry: He saved others, himself he cannot save.

Concerning the use of the word to heal.

The word of power to heal must be of a positive nature, expressive only of good, or beauty, or health, or blessedness, and in no way negative, or affording consideration or recognition to the symptoms of disorder.

It may be a word of the most childlike simplicity, and indeed I should say that in such would be expressed the greater power.

Thus have I been allowed to relieve a gentle sufferer from pain of body and to enliven the whole nature by simply continuing to utter in the silence to her soul this word as it arose and kept repeating itself in me, "Jesu's little lovie;" and her nurse, who is sufficiently enlightened to understand, and to whom I gave the word, uses it now unfailingly with beautiful and wondrous results

For the soul receives such a word most easily, and no soul to whom you would address such a word in her need would reject it, if only it is uttered in the power of the great quiet and in the silence of self.

The soundless word for such a use is always the more potent.

The great thing, so far as personal effort is concerned, is to persevere in uttering the word, and not to allow weariness of mind or body to overcome your will of blessing in the service.

And so the use of the word must not depend on how we feel at the time; for to be subject to our feelings, as we know so well, not only robs us of many a genuine opportunity of doing the good thing, but in time actually paralyses our power of doing or saying the good thing. We must use the word given us to use, whatever may be the mood of the moment, knowing it to be a word of power.

There is here certainly a need for this exhortation, for the finer vessels of the healing Christ are always of the idealistic or artistic temperament; and we know that here is the snare and here is the infirmity of this highly-wrought type, even to be subject to the domination of feeling or the power of appearances.

And all our experiences in life are meant to bring forth in us the power to be free from the dominion of these passing states of consciousness.

Concerning Limitations.

There is so much wisdom in the old word, "The merciful man regardeth the life of his beast." And this animal nature and this human body is a good servant, and we must never be unmindful of its limitations and its temperamental needs.

We must be kind to our little animal; we must consider the beast of burden that has borne us so willingly and so well through our present life.

For we wrong this willing soul if we force, or try to force her in any way.

By refusing to recognise these limitations as essentially in and of our present nature we violate the holy will or law of life. And we suffer for the sin.

And the penalty is that the sweet bouquet of the Pleroma, the gentle beauty of God, the fragrance of the holy Child, the fine aroma which makes men desire for or love us, is not generated in, and cannot be shed through our nature, but must withdraw herself from us; and we are left barren of blessedness, without "presence" and unwanted by the soul of man. Let us attain to be human, truly, wholly human, before we claim to be divine, for thus only do we become in reality divine in our whole nature.

✠ ✠ ✠

There is nothing so practical as the wisdom of the one great seer, Love. It is for all our needs the very wisdom of God.

And so to you, my most near and dear companions in the great work of breaking and giving the Bread to the little children of Christ, let me, as one who has suffered much through an unrestrained zeal for the health of this human house of God, counsel you, when the exhaustion of your personal forces are clearly manifest through weariness and the desire to go apart and rest awhile, just to yield to this quiet suggestion of nature. For it is the still, small voice of your own holy Lover, who is calling your nature in her desire for rest, to come away with Love and be quiet for a time beside the still waters and amid the green pastures of the one blessedness wherein is your only true recreation and refreshing.

For the unwillingness to do so is in all likelihood of the will of the anxious old self, in whom assuredly is the source of all our pains and miseries, even unto these nerval breakdowns so common now among the ardent workers for good.

But when at last we yield up all this blind old self-will, who foolishly imagines that the work of God is his work, and withdraw our whole nature into the deep quiet of the one will of blessing, then we shall rest for a season, and in the fulness of time we shall find that a new power, ever finer and fuller, has been imparted to us, that once more the song of Life is singing within us and more sweetly, that the vision of God is restored to our soul, and that she sees more deeply into the mystery of Beauty than heretofore. This I have never known to fail, either in my own experience or in that of any others, and I give this assurance to you, my zealous companions in service, for it cannot fail to serve your health.*

Indeed, comrades, it is well worth our while to listen to and obey the call of the great Lover.

Healing in the Spirit, wherein is the use and touch of the Personal Soul.

One of the most interesting modes of this spiritual healing, and these modes are many, is when you are led to visit the little ones one by one, giving to each soul just what the Diagnoser in you finds at the time to be its need.

This service also is usually fulfilled in or through me during the very early hours of the morning.

And thus we are led to begin. We go to the north of Scotland and visit those whose call we feel.

We are then in conscious possession of a live organ or vessel through which we conduct to this one the fluid or essence of Life. We often find the body asleep, and the soul is thus ready to receive the food.

And then it is just as if you were gently spraying or pouring a fine liquid-food into these souls. And you can feel the little child absorbing it, and you can sense the eagerness of the soul in so drinking.

And you can feel the various qualities of essences that are thus administered to each and several soul, and these correspond to their present need and to the service of health that the spirit wills to do unto each at this time.

For it is not merely for the service of health in any narrow sense that this work is done, but it may be as truly for a domestic or personal comfort, through direction or inspiration, or even correction and reproof.

* Never believe dear fellow-worker, that stimulation can take the place of recreation. This is a very common delusion. When weariness overtakes your nature seek rest or quiet of body or mind in preference even to food or any stimulant.

Thus do we go from one to another, from north to south of our land, using the knowledge we have of those who need and are ready for the service; and thus do we administer the holy love-substance to those who do look to get it through us.

Well do we know when one is waiting and ready for it, because it is at once received, and there is no obstacle whatsoever to the efflux.

And thus we pass beyond the oceans, and also visit the little children in the ends of the earth; and, inasmuch as time and space are not here, they too receive what is good for them.

This whole service may last for one or two or more hours, according to the resources and powers of the personal vessel at the time.

As you will see clearly, it is really a very heavy service for the whole nature of the ministrant.

For the personal touch is in it, and all the powers of the personal will, or desire and knowledge, are used in it.

Yet are they used in a mode that is altogether super-personal in nature, in effect, and in issue.

But it is, all the same, a strain on the human vessel, and psyche is thankful to be called away at last from it into the highland auras and divine airs of the purely super-personal degrees, wherein she re-enters the service and fellowship of the inner and unnumbered company, and where she always finds rest.

In this service, as in all others, we know that the power, being of God, is unlimited, but we also know that this channel, vessel, or organon is limited. And were we, as so many earnest souls are apt to do, to forget this fact, we shall soon be reminded of it by our experience.

And this too is only for our health, for to be mindful of the limitations of our vessel keeps us humble; and to be humble, sweetly humble, is to be in the sanity of Christ.

The Dissipating of the Clouds of Self.

The Sun of the soul is always shining, but at times the mists, clouds, and miasmas of the lower self or earth nature hide over the face of our Holy One, and so he cannot shine forth for our blessedness. And the work of healing is then to blow away these mists from the soul of anyone we would serve.

And this work is done by the breathing forth of Love on that soul, breathing and breathing the Holy Thing until these mists are all blown away by the strength, and these miasmas are all consumed away by the heat of the Great Sun in the soul.

Healing through a Body not in Physical Health.

Have you, my sister, my brother dear in the service of the healing Christ, ever observed that, according to the very general testimony of the recipients, the finest virtue that has been shed through you may have been in the very deepest of your personal pain or darkness, or anguish of soul, or it may be, of body? Is it not, that the great work of the oblation or sacrifice of self unto Love is even now being fulfilled in you literally and actually in and through your nature whose vital elements are being consumed in the fire of the great Soul-service, and that all this strange experience is only an answer to the most earnest prayer of your whole nature when she cried out in the power of the great self-giving will of Love: "Here am I, O Lord of Love, be pleased, if thou wilt, to use me even as I am."

For let it be understood that the *summum bonum* of Life is not physical health, but wholeness or harmony of the powers of mind and soul and body.

We can and do make far too much of the mere physical as a good, and this leads us to speak of a very interesting theme, viz., the work of healing through a body not in health.

✠ ✠ ✠

Now I know that this is a fact, for I have myself experienced it so often and seen it working in others, and besides, the lives of the saints abound in stories of such work.

I know a gentle sufferer who has lain on her bed for six years now, and I can vouch for it, that the power of healing, yes, of actual, physical healing, has increased in her soul as the health of her body has decreased.

The explanation of this is in the whole doctrine of the transmutation of the elemental powers into a degree of a finer and higher potency through the service of pain, of which I have spoken very fully in the Song of the Cross and in the Crucifixion and Resurrection of the Christ of Germany.

And the suffering soul may thus become so sensitive that it can serve in a way and where another equally willing servant of Life cannot serve.

I have noticed that the health of the body and the mind of the nurse not only keeps well but has much improved while caring for her and sleeping in the sick-room all these years.

Indeed, I am very sure that most serious services of life, which we robust people little dream of, are fulfilled through the fine or delicate body of "the invalid."

Perhaps I should say that though well on in years, the personality of this sufferer becomes more and more of the heaven-born child. She is the good cheer and the very joy-spring of the whole house. The atmosphere of that room is so sweet with the live presence of the angels of God that her friends desire nothing so much as just to be allowed to sit there even though it be in silence.

The Power of blessing ceaseth never.

Now this holy Thing is not always in outer, active operation, *i.e.*, you, in your external consciousness, cannot always be in the joy of its activity. For there are periods when the bodies through which it manifests in your outer and inner consciousness must rest, and it withdraws itself into the innermost or holy place of your being so that these bodies may rest.

But there it is not inactive, for it ceases never from its work. In fact, it has only withdrawn to its own place of power, and there, even while you as a mundane consciousness may be feeling that you are doing nothing of good, and when, in very fact, you may be only able to lie still, it is working in the finest and highest of the spiritual potencies, and bringing forth then, even through your own unified will of blessing, such fruits of its own pure power as may well be, in actual realization, beyond the range of your ordinary mundane comprehension to measure.

And this is done through your whole ego or unified personal consciousness, because you are now altogether in your elements given unto and in the power of the one will of blessing.

This word of truth is of so great a comfort to many of the most gentle, beautiful, and lowly of Christ's little children that I feel I cannot give it too frequently nor in too many or varying modes of expression for their special service.

✠ ✠ ✠

Now once this holy one has wholly become in you the actual power of Life, it needs neither to be coaxed nor to be forced to work the work of blessing in and through you. For it is, as we have said, the ceaseless worker in your nature, and will never fail, because it is the worker, to use all the vital energies of your body and of your soul that it is well in Life, and according to the law of God in you, for it to use now as at any time.

Of this fact you need have no doubt whatsoever, nor of the truth herein implied, that it will never use your nature to her hurt; for how can God in you violate the will of Life, the law of God?

Hence it is that I never either try to force its activity in myself, nor by coaxing seek to draw it forth into manifestation in another soul who is, I know, equally given over to the will of blessing.

For I have learned through much painful experience that it is wrong to do so.

For, let us repeat, there are times when it is well to be still. The physical and super-physical vessels or bodies of activity need it so; and our holy one knows this, and being the very Genius of the Great Compassion, is merciful to his own creature of limited capacity.

And there are seasons when it is well, for the very sake of the work that is being done within the great deep of our nature, to keep quiet in every sense of the word; and to ignore or violate these clear intimations of our holy nature is to sin through self-will the sin of intemperance. For we can be intemperate or greedy in the service of the good or beautiful as truly as in the pursuit of the evil or ugly. And for the health of the most ardent lovers of the house of God, even the body of our creation, it is indeed well that this vital truth be not forgotten.

I do not say that this is necessarily so, but I know that it is not at all an unlikely experience to the more sensitive of us, and especially to those who are strong in the poetic or prophetic modes of forthgoing.

But you need really experience no distress through this sense of lack, for all you have to do is to bide quiet, and waiting patiently on God, just allow the Blessedness to refill your vessel; and, when you know that this is unfailingly so, you will allow it to be done in you, even you, human soul, the servant of God; and you will know no evil.*

Concerning the Sending Forth of the Power of Healing.

Be it well noted that so long as there is any conscious effort of self-will in the act of the forth-sending of power, it is yet in the psychic realm, and is therefore, however beautiful in operation and sweet in desire, subject to the aberrations and limitations of this realm, such as depletion of vitality and other personal hurt, *e.g.* being infected of the evil and being made subject to its influence in your soul, or mind, or flesh.

Therefore I counsel my companions in this the most holy act of Christ-power, knowing that the Living One is ever here, waiting, waiting, just to serve in and through us, to say to the Holy Presence—"Now I am Thy vessel; my whole nature is the servant of Thy will; use me, even as Thou willest."

---

* When the soul is thus rapt in God, *i.e.* consciously one, in and with the Holy Being of Life, she becomes the vessel of the highest power for the transmission of the health of God throughout the whole of our personal nature even unto the outermost degree.

I do not speak here of the trance state, although I know that what I say is equally true of that state, for I have not in this life had any experience of that state.

And so it is that she fulfils, when in this most intense super-conscious degree of being, the greatest service for the health of the personal nature, nor in any way by the conscious effort of the self-will, but simply and naturally as the normal fruition of this vital conscious union with God.

During this state all sense of personal limitation and of physical or psychic discomfort such as the feeling of cold or misery passes away, for she is in God where Life alone is, and she consciously is of God who is Life.

It may be of use here to add that in this super-personal service there is no need for objects of psychometric contact such as letters, rings, etc. I know the use of such and they are all good in their own way and degree, but they are certainly not needed here.

Need I say here that this rule of power operates equally in all the modes of healing wherein the genius of our personality is used, from the laying on of hands to the speaking of the soundless word?

And thus it is that we can send forth, in the will of the Giver of all good, the power of any sweet or beautiful experience we are enjoying, saying thus: "Take now, I pray thee, the beauty, the joy, the sweetness of this present delight of my nature, take it and give it unto whomsoever can, in their need, now receive it."

And even though this good be in itself of a psychic or sensuous or physical nature, the desire that it be given to the needy one sanctifies it and gives to it a power of spiritual blessing that will surely bear it to its goal.

And you can know when it has gone and when it has been received; for this is the forth-sending of the virtue of the body of the Lord of Life.

And if the service of any one be given to you to fulfil at the time of your *jouissance*, it may be a use to keep repeating the name of this one while you are in this conscious enjoyment of the beauty, for thus the soul you would serve is drawn into and kept in the power of the beauty of God, and so blest.

Of this you may be sure, that if only you have been enabled thus to make of your nature a whole vessel of God, if you have made unto Love the utter oblation of self in all her desires and wills, you can enter into any service in any possible mode of healing, how trying soever it may be to the personal nature, without the slightest risk of any hurt of any kind.

For there is now no element of the old selfhood found to be positively aworking here, and so there is no *point d'apport* or place of power for the evil thing so to contact as to gain a ground in you to contaminate you.

This, dear companions in the Christ-nature, is a sure,

sure doctrine, and for our personal health and comfort it is well worthy of our most serious thought and practice.

Concerning the Self-Will in Christ Healing.

The healer in Christ has come to where the soul ceases from all effort of self-will. He knows that soon as she is set free from all desire born in self, even unto the desire for the realising of the will to bless, she becomes a live vessel into whom the living God can flow, and through whom the Holy One can give itself freely and fully to all who are seeking after it.

And so he is now able to silence all the voices of self, however good in their own degree and realm they be, and to say to the Holy One of Life: "Thy will alone; thy power alone; yea, thou and thou alone." And this is the whole of will that now works in this soul, and it is the will of God. And so she is verily in the great work, and the Great Worker is working in and through this maiden body of God.

And she, the servant, is at rest now, for she has come into all her own estate, even all the good of the living God.

And she knows no more desire for any good thing, for she is all in Christ who is the fulness of all the good of Life.

No craving to know, no yearning now to do even the works of the will of blessing; no more hunger and thirst after righteousness; for Christ, the whole Blessedness of God, is in her, ay more truly in and of her than any element or personal power of her nature; even Christ, the sweet Indweller, the Lover, the Giver of all good; Christ the Healer, the ever-radiating Sun of her blessedness; Christ, the whole Beauty of God, is now her inalienable possession, her eternal all and in all.

Need I say that as a sure fruition of this estate, the

healer in Christ will never allow any little child to look to him personally as the healer, and nothing would offend more this human vessel than that it should be so esteemed.

And his great work will always be to point the little one to its own Healing Christ, and his unchanging word will always be: Not in this man, not in this woman-vessel is thy healing, but in thine own ever-present, living Christ-lover.

And thus, as I have already written and more fully in "The Christ of the Healing Hand," the truly spiritual healer is supremely a liberator of the soul, and cannot but work for the one supreme good of psyche, even her freedom from all bonds, her conscious enjoyment of her eternal birthright, the inviolable liberty to be her own true self, to use her own free-will.

These words have come to us for our use; and we give them now to you for any use they may be to you, the lover and the servant of the Body of Christ.

The word of the great oblation.

O Christ, hast thou not made thy suffering, even thine, O serving Lover of our creation, my one, my only good?

How then, knowing this so well, can I turn me away from any suffering?

Nay, nay, I shall turn me from none. Too precious is it to be denied; too great its virtue to be missed.

And so I am now willing to bear in my soul or in my flesh all the suffering of this little one.

And because I am able to bear it, and thy little child is not able, I ask thee to allow me to bear the power of it in my body, or in my soul, or in my mind, or in whatever way thou, O Master, O Lover, seest fit to transmute its power into my estate.

☩ ☩ ☩

Every soul who is in the service of the whole will of blessing, ever bears about as in her very arms some little one, some darling child of her compassion—it may be a man or a woman of years, it may be anyone whose very feebleness of body, or soul, or mind, renders it the darling of your tenderest love.

And this little one, being the child of your compassion, is thus in very reality the child of the One of great Compassion, even the soul of the Christ-mother.

And when at last you do realise the truth that this little one is not yours but Christ's own, is not the supreme act of self-renunciation, even the utter yielding up of the Christ of this little one, also the supreme act of the divine or love-wisdom in you for the little one then?

Indeed it cannot be otherwise, for who as the Christ-mother can care for her own little child?

The offering of the whole nature to the Service of Love.

O Christ, thou hast given me all, all these little ones to care for, even as thine own little children, the very lambs of thy great flock.

This I know if there is aught I know; for thou hast given me thine own mother-love, and thou hast made me to love them all in this very will of thine own blessing.

And I know that this is the greatest boon that thy love can give to this human soul, to make me, even me, this child of these crude elements, the servant of thy most needy little ones.

And, knowing thy gift to be so, I vow to thee that so long as the power of this body endures I shall not fail to do thy will of blessing unto any and every human soul who through the voice of her need calls unto me for the service of Love.

And I know that this great gift of thy service ceases not in any way with the power of this body or of this animal soul, but that in the new body which thou art preparing for me I shall continue to fulfil this thine own will of blessing in an ever-increasing power of Love.

And my soul ceases not night nor day in her prayer to thee that she may ever be found worthy, truly worthy of the service, so that thy power in her may never, never fail. And she knows that thy power in her can not fail, yet ceases she never from the prayer of her great desire.

The word of the unfailing Good Cheer, being the admonition of the ever-living Christ of the soul to the little one who would wear itself away and consume its strength in vain regrets for the errors of the past.

O child of the ages, O fruit of many lives, without beginning and without ending art thou, even thou; for thou art my own child, being of my being, substance of my substance.

There is no place in all thy past where I have not been. Through all these strange ways have I walked with thee, and I have never been away from thee, neither in thy nights nor in thy days.

And all these experiences have been needful to thee. Not one of them which has not been the servant of thy good, not one of them from which thou hast not learned a lesson or drawn an enduring strength.

Thus the past is thine; it is all in thee, and it hath served thee well.

And now, O my child, is not the present thine, and is not the future equally thine, yea more so, for from these past ways thou hast learned how best to use every forthgoing of thy life for the service of the other soul, even of whomsoever needs thy love?

And thou art now able to do with it thus and ever as is thy desire; for I am in thee and of thee, yea essentially thee, even unto the ages of thy lives.

And soon as Love is perfect in thee, there is no more sin, nor any record thereof in Life.

And, the desire of thy heart being right with me, thou hast already washed clean thy robes from all these stains.

Yea I am, yea I am, yea I am; and I am thy sweetness, thy health, thy joy, and all the beauty that the soul of man, or angel, or beast can desire to see in thee, O child of my blessedness unto the ages of ages.

The response of the Soul to the holy Indweller, and the vow of her love.

I know, O my holy One, that thou hast come to dwell in me. I know that thou art thus making my life thy life and thy life my life.

And so I know that it is indeed well with me, and cannot but be well henceforth and for evermore.

And now for thine own sake, and because of the great Love that hath made thy life my life, I shall be pure and sweet and strong in love; and worthy, and ever more worthy of thy fellowship, my friend, my lover, my heartmate, sun of my day, star of my night.

The Faith and the Prayer of the Faith of the soul to the Holy Indweller.

I know, O my Holy One, that thou art able to make me whole, and I know that thou art making me whole.

I know, O my Sweetness of Life, that thou art making me cleaner and sweeter in the inward parts.

I know, O my Lover, that thou art making me more and more loving and true and gentle.

I know, O my Beautiful One, that thou art saving me from all my olden unworthiness by making me more and more beautiful through and through, and more and more worthy to be the servant of Love.

I know that it is in order to give me thy health that thou hast come to be the light of this man.

I know that thou art born in me, making thus thy home in my nature, just to give me all thy sweet health; and I know, O Saviour-lover, that thou art now dwelling in me in order to give me thy whole beauty; and I ask thee to draw me and ever draw me until I am all absorbed into thy Beauty.

And in the name of this Holy Love I vow to be a dweller in the heart of the human need, there to give of all the best of my life for her health, even as thou hast given the power of all thy beauty for my salvation.*

To the Good Hand

(*For the service of the power to renounce all personal care*).

O Hand of God, O good Hand, into thy keeping we now commit all, all, all who are a care to our human soul, and we cease from all anxiety concerning them.

O Hand of God, O good Hand, we commit to thee now our own nature and all we are and all our ways and activities in life. For even the health of this body we have made thy care, and we have no fear however strange and "alarming" symptoms may arise in our nature. And we cease from all care about our past our present or our future.

Surely, surely, O Christ, we know thee well. Surely we know thee to be the Hand of God and all the power thereof for us. Surely it is well to let thee do all for us and in us. Surely, O Christ, we can leave all with thee now.

And, having committed all to thee, no more need we to pray unto thee for any good, for that were to return to the past infirmity. And so, even as a little child rests in the arms of the mother's love, we shall rest

* *Salus* means health, hence salvation.

in thine arms and thus draw all these thy little ones into the deep quiet of thy peace wherein is the health of God, the only health. For until we have committed our all unto thee and made thee our whole good we have not entered into life the blsssed.

The Angel-Healer.

The strength, the efficiency and the live and fine art of the healer is in the power to see the angel in any soul. For the angel of good in any soul is none other than this same Christ-Spirit, even the Holy One of this nature. And in all the servants of Life, whatever be the mode of their service, this is the One who serves.

And in as much as this One uses our psyche, limited and imperfect as she is in herself, it is well in our judgment of our fellow-worker that we always differentiate between this Holy One of the nature and the personality whom it uses as the body or vessel of service. Thus our judgment will be just and in the kindly wisdom of the love who considers and bears all things.

In some this Beautiful One is more manifest than in others. Sure as you have met that soul or really looked into that eye you see it. And it too sees your Angel, and knows at once that your Christ or the lover in you recognises and loves it. And henceforth you are friends, comrades, ay, lovers.

For it is the Angel-Christ or Lover in you who alone can see and recognise the Holy One in another soul. And the stronger, maturer or finer the body of the Angel-Christ in you be, the swifter and surer is your power to see and recognise and love.

And the power to see the Angel is the power to call it forth, and the power to call it forth is the power to heal in the only mode worthy to be called Christ-healing. And to be in, and to use this power is the one true and only spiritual healing known to me.

For, once the Christ in you has touched and spoken to the Christ in the other soul, this Angel-Christ is quickened and awakened into the self-consciousness of its present actuality, and the great work of healing is begun in that nature, working ever in and through the psyche, and ultimating, if it be well so to ultimate, even in the renewing of the physique.

And this Holy One will not cease from working the great work of Life in and through the soul or psyche until all that nature is made whole through and through and altogether beautiful in the health of God.

Awake, O sleeping One.

So speaks the Christ of your soul to the sleeping Christ of the soul of the patient.

For the Christ or Divine Energizer has not yet awakened in this soul unto self-consciousness out of the deep sleep into which it willingly merged itself when it clothed itself in our animal nature for the redemption of this soul from the grave of materiality.

And if we are awake and truly alive in our own divinity, and fully conscious of the power of our own living Sun, we can, in that power, awaken the Christ of the soul of our brother unto the consciousness of its own divine potency, saying thus to it:

Awake, O Sun, awake, thou who here sleepest the heavy sleep of materiality; awake to newness of Life, and Christ, even the Holy Sun, the Spiritual Light of this cosmos, will give thee Life.

Awake in this soul, O strong Son of God, arise, come forth in thy might, and the Great Christ, thy Holy Sun of Blessing, will give thee Life.

A word of promission for the use of all Lovers.

O thou who art the strength of my flesh and of my blood, of my will and of my mind, give now, I pray thee, of thy virtue to this feeble little child.

O Fragrance, sweet fragrance of the health of my whole nature, breathe, O breathe thyself through and through the garments of this feeble soul, cleansing and sweetening and vivifying them now with thy life.

O my holy one, thou who art the light of my soul and the star of her reason, keeping her ever, throughout the ages of her journeyings in all the modes of her being, one and the same, give, O give the joy of thy light and the serenity of thy vision to this darkened mind.

O Sun, radiant sun of my heart, shine now, I pray thee, into the despondency of this soul bechilled of the damp miasmas of death, pour into her thy warmth and thy cheer, consuming these mists and shining away these clouds of doubt and gloom.

O Jesu, love of my heart, my own, my best, my nearest friend, give, O give thy love, thy whole love, and all the sweetness and joy thereof unto this little one, weary and afflicted with the sorrows of this land of shadows.

Freely, freely I give thee to this hungry child, dying for lack of love, that she too, poor, famishing soul, may be satisfied with thy beauty.

O Christ, living Christ of my soul, thou who art my one beauty, my sole excellency, my whole goodness, yea, my all and in all, give, O give thy power of life and all the beauty and all the goodness thereof, now, even now, unto the poorest, uncomeliest and most miserable who can receive the blessing, whosoever and wheresoever this soul be.

Great may be the joy, sure certainly is the comfort of this forthgoing to the soul who thus fulfils it, even as the comfort of all true service is sure.

Yet when the service has been actually fulfilled through your nature, you must not be surprised to find that a sense of emptiness, or it may even be, a painful feeling of lack or lowness follows or may follow in due course.*

* But here again let us note well that when the forth-sending or forth-going is not in any way of your personal will, but of the one will, even the will of God in whom your whole nature is now hid, immersed, or absorbed, the power of healing is so immeasurably finer and greater as to be of another order altogether, and this is so because that is yet in and of your self-will, and, while altogether good in kind, is only of the human degree with all its necessary limitations and imperfections, while this mode is of the Divine order and is clothed in the power and inbreathed of the very Christ of your nature, and is subject never to sense of lack or pain.

☩ ☩ ☩

That the Healer in us is actually and in very fact as a living sun has been well proved to me through varied testimony concerning the work of healers.

Of one of these testimonies I shall speak because it concerns my own work as a healer, and because I have known most intimately for years the lady who testifies, and she is one of the clearest, finest and most matter of fact intelligences known to me.

Now she has always declared, and this before I myself fully realised the siginificance of the phenomenon, that what she recognises as my sun comes to her in the work of healing, and that its appearance is always according to the degree of the healing power as it manifests in and through my spiritual nature. Does this sun appear to be feeble? Then the healing power is feeble; Is the appearance that of a greater radiance? Then the healing power is greater, and so on.

But when I explained to her that it was not my sun nor I who was shining, but Christ, the one living Sun who was shining through my spiritual nature, that it is His light and warmth and not mine; and when she fully realised this end accordingly ceased to look to this man but as the body of manifestation, the blessing or power of healing was so increased in her and for her that she is now a conscious radiator of the power of the living Sun, and thus working with her own Christ in the work of the will of blessing.

These Addenda are inscribed to the honour of the Love of our Philemon and Baucis.

My intention was to print this in a separate booklet but it will serve you better to have them here now.

During a recent visit to a Yorkshire town, I was the honoured guest at the breakfast table of a most worthy couple, who, because of the gentle beauty of their years, their simple and truly childlike ways, and their loyal love to one another, I have named Philemon and Baucis.

For the King of the gods, even Christ the holy Lover, has indeed visited this lowly human home, and out of all their common cares and the common triumph of love over them all, has won for them the immortal beauty of the ageless Youth.

And because at their chaste and frugal table we three have daily broken the bread of Life, and fulfilled in one soul the most holy sacrament of the communal Love-feast, I inscribe this little book of Love talks to these two little children of our one Father-Mother in God, even the Christ of the Ages of our race.

For this is indeed the work of the Great Lover in my nature for your health, and who but Love can give you and me, human soul, the eternal youth of the Health of God?

And who but the one living Sun of our humanity can infuse into the child of this earth the immortal beauty of the ageless gods?

Ay, Christ, our Christ alone, the holy Love-Spirit in you, dear soul, as in me, can make us and keep us eternally young; for Love, Love and Love alone, is the very power and sap and substance of the Youth whose bloom passeth never away.

My sister, my brother, you have seen this live Beauty in others. Do you actually possess it now? Answer your soul in truth. For if she says to you, "No," then believe me your lover in God, it is waiting there now, even in your human nature, for realization.

N.B.—I make no descent and offer no apology to pure art for the service of the health of your body, for surely this is the service of the Lord of Life, and in all my writings I seek to fulfil it.

For our Philemon is a born *cordon bleu*, and his genius has, even in these hungry days, daily fed my body right well on a substantial porridge of half oat and half maize, which, in honour due to the discoverer, I have named the Philemon mixture. As with all such foods, it is well to cook it stiff and solid. Steep the maize overnight. Give it a trial. It will serve your body well.

By the way, read what I have written in "Brotherhood of Healers, p. 58, on the use of these most succulent fruits of the earth, —usually discarded by the gardener,—young sprouts of cabbage, turnips, etc.

Concerning the Great Communal Service of Healing.

For long time now I have known and have often declared that my work as a healer in Christ has really been removed from the exterior to the interior realm of being. It is, for example, no longer the delight for me to talk publicly of these things that it has been in the past. Indeed, to tell true, for some good time now it is to me more or less a weariness so to do.

But, on the other hand, when I am called into the service of the inner light, into the fellowship and power of pure spirit, and allowed to work where the personal, in its usual denotation, is transcended, I am indeed in my own place of power, and I know that I am doing there the best service that can now be done in and through my nature.

And this is so in very fact with so many now, that I feel I could not do better for these our high-born sisters and brothers in life and for the great service of healing, than just give the few words that I am now able to give towards their guidance, enlightening, efficiency, and good cheer in the fulfilling of their own most holy Christ-will of blessing.

Concerning the sitting together.

It is good to come together as companions or fellows in life for the fulfilling of this service, for then it is a communal service, and so the one living Bread of the communion feast is never wanting. In form it is really of the nature of the Quakers' silent meeting, only that there seems to us to be a higher practicality in its genuius, inasmuch as its will is given consciously to the service of the need of the other rather than to the service of the need of self.

✠   ✠   ✠

And now, when we are thus together in the one Presence, and in the physical presence of each other, and we are moved to send forth the Power of the Holy One of our nature, it may be, and usually is given us to use, in the silence of the soul, some word of Power, whether it be a name for our own most familiar Holy One, such as Jesus, or Christ, or Krishna, or Buddha, or Hari, or the name of your guru or guide, friend or master, incarnate or decarnate, for all such are in the One whom we name the Great Christ of our Cosmos, and who for us transcends all our names. And it may be the name of some spiritual essence, such as Peace, or Love, or Beauty, or Joy, or the simple word "Blessing," than which I know of no more potent word for general use, for implies the whole presence of God.

And it matters not though your name be not the same in sound as the name of the brother who sits beside you, for all these varying sounds, coming forth in the pure spontaneity of the Holy Presence, are one in essence and power, and are as notes in the many chords of the Great Harmony of Life, forming the one live Word of the Christ-Presence and uttering all the power thereof; and if we are in the consciousness of the One it is the power and only the power of the One in them we invoke.*

Indeed, as I have already told my readers, it suffices to keep uttering the Holy Name of Blessing, while you are in the healing afflatus or power, in order that it go to the one you now desire to serve in life.

Thus do we sit together in the power of the one great Lord and Healer, and whether we have come in the human desire for the fulfilling of some personal need, or in the great desire of the Giver of all our good to the other, we are all invited and exhorted to make the great oblation of our whole nature even now and here unto the One Lover and Healer, saying thus—"Here am I just as I am—use me even as thou seest best, for I offer unto Thee now all that I am."

It is made known by word, that in our human nature is this divine prerogative, that she can say, if she is in the full use of her normal powers—"I will to love; I will to serve; and I shall now love and serve freely, wholly, universally."

And inasmuch as she makes the unreserved offering of her whole strength, or virtue, ay, how poor soever she feels it to be, she is there and then accepted of the One Lover and Healer, ordained of the only Hand that can ordain unto any spiritual love-service, and becomes in her own degree one of the unnumbered

---

* This use of names or words we give for those to whom it is a use. But in the whole Light there is no name, only the sense of the One who is nameless. For, as already said elsewhere, the great word of power is uttered in the soundless deep of the soul, where no name is or can be uttered. For our vessel is then, in her super-consciousness, consciously one with the One.

The use of names, as of all words, we leave to the genius of the healer, and it is best so. And all our suggestions towards the use of words are meant to be so received by the companions, who are indeed of many creeds, yet one in the love of God and in the power of the holy name. And so, while the other is truly a good in certain stages, it remains best in our seeing, when circumstances allow it, to name only the One. And this we have always suggested to those who need or desire the use of a name. And to us no word or sound of a name utters so well the whole fulness or very nearness of the One as "Jesu-Christ."

companions of the great Brotherhood of Healers incarnate and decarnate, whose decarnate members we name the body of the Ascension into power of the Lord of Life, or the risen body of Christ.

☩ ☩ ☩

This is the great and holy fellowship into which, through the love-gift of herself, even as she is, the human soul is now introduced. And so she becomes partaker in their foods, and in their powers, and in all the fine beauties and uses thereof.

And this is her initiation into the service of the temple of the Health of God. Thus does the sister or brother who has come as a seeker only of a personal good, become a participant in the service, and thus a recipient of the greatest possible good for the health of the body, or of the soul.

The Body of this Service.

Concerning the constitution of this body of communal Love-service, I have already spoken fully in "The Christ of the Healing Hand" (see p. 128), so that my words here need be few. Let me say, in passing, that I here use the word "Companion," as it best expresses the essential relationship of all the participants in the service, being derived from "com" and "panis," literally meaning "together in or with bread."

Now, inasmuch as it is a body whose elements are of earth and heaven, *i.e.* of the incarnate sitters and their decarnate fellows or companions, the real Presence or personal Power of the Great Healer cannot fail to enter it, for sure as the body of service is prepared for Me, so surely do I come into this body. And in very fact this Presence never, never fails, nor the power thereof. And this is well known to all who truly participate in the service.

It is well and beautiful at this period of the service to name some of the many whom we know to be present with us in the spirit, though not in the body. And, as in this service there is no distinction whatever between the incarnate and the decarnate, we name equally our companions in this body and our arisen comrades. This is a service of the holy human affections, for many are in both these degrees of life who love to know that they are thus named.

It may be of a use then to sing together a song of the healing Love, or of the Great Peace, for we believe in the use of the holy note for the unifying of the elements of this communal body of service, and of this we shall speak more fully hereafter.

For just as much as we realise that this work is in no way in or of our personal will or power, that it is not our work, but God's own work, that these little ones are not our care but Christ's own care, is our psyche set free to become the vessel of the one

Power. And this great principle, as I have said elsewhere, runs right through the work of healing in all its modes, and is as vital to its efficiency in the outer as in the inner degree of this service.

The Naming of any who Desire to be Named.

And now that the vessel is formed and made ready for use in all her parts and powers, we invite all those present, as our fellows in service, to name by initial letter, pet-name, Christian name, or otherwise, even as it is convenient unto them, any whom they feel moved to name for their participation in this service of the health of God.

For you cannot name any soul in this present consciousness of the presence without thereby bringing it into live contact with the power of the Presence that it needs for its health.

And it cannot fail to receive the one touch of the Healing Christ, and this touch is as true seed deposited in its nature, which seed will certainly ultimate in the fulness of time in the health of body, or of mind, or of any other personal power, or principle, or element.

☦ ☦ ☦

Yet, though a good, it is not a necessary service so to name, for all they whom we could or should name are recorded in the book of our heart, and these are seen and known to the Reader of the heart and the Prover of our love.

And, indeed, there are always the one or two or several whom, because of personal intimacy, or for some delicate reason of our nature, we cannot well name, and never do name in public. They are the very near darlings of our human nature, the little ones whom the Christ-mother hath, in a special way, given us to nurture and comfort or care for in her name and for her sake.

We all know who these are. Every soul of service has such, and she alone knows them and can name them in the place of her power, even in the hearing of the Ear who heareth every desire and in the sight of the Eye who seeth every word of the prayer too deep, too live, too strong in yearning to be uttered in speech articulate.

And so we give now a silent time to this most gentle love-service, closing this period with the openly declared yielding up of these our most cherished and precious charges into the hands of the Will who doeth all things well, knowing that for their service, as for the service of all, we can never do better than so to yield them, to commit them truly and utterly into the keeping of the one great Father-Mother-Lover of us all. And surely it is well for those, the most cherished of our nature, that we do so, for knows not the great Love better than we, how best to serve their whole good?

And that we do so really and utterly yield them up, is indeed a triumph of the holy Will in our nature, and it cannot but bear to them a more abundant and blessed fruit in life than could possibly be borne through the labour and effort of our personal will and sense of possession, which very possession actually interferes with the healing of the child of our personal labour, as we know so well, often because of its anxiety and sense of care. And so the best word of committal for these, as for all we would serve in life, must ever be: "For they are Thine own little ones, and not ours; and we are for them only the servants of thy will."

And with such a word we close this most sacred period of our service.

Concerning the Service of Some Present Social Need.

There is always some special call from the need of the social body for the service of our communal body of healing.

Thus, *e.g.* in these days of air-raids we do well to devote a period of our time to the service of the thousands of panic-stricken, fearful little children of Christ in our midst. And we are well assured that here indeed we have been allowed to fulfil a very vital and most important national service.

To this end we find it a good thing to sing together a song of the Omnipresence, or a hymn of trust, the companions in service being reminded that we sing this not for the comfort of our own need, though verily we too cannot fail to be most abundantly blessed in singing it with full intent and desire for the comforting of these fearful, little children.

And to this end our fellow-ministrants are asked to enter the state of these souls, and allow themselves to be merged in them and in their need while singing the hymn of trust, for thus they sing the strength of their faith in God, not only *unto* these feeble and needy souls, but actually *in* them, so that they may feel that the power of faith is being born in their own nature. Thus is fulfilled the service of a great and pressing need of the hour, and they who fulfil it know from its actual beauty that it is verily a service whole and efficient in the power of the healing Presence of the Lord of Life.

Or it may be that we are moved to fulfil the service of blessing specially for those who have been taken suddenly and violently out of their young bodies through this war.

And we speak to these the great gospel of Life by affirming that no soul can ever be lost unto the Christ, for the love of God encompasseth every soul whosoever and wheresoever that soul be.

Now, as heretofore said, having made the great oblation of self in all her powers, we have been received and used accordingly in the great service of the body of the Lord of Life.

For thus used we are actually in our heaven of blessedness,

i.e. in the best of our true estate and in the full use of all the powers thereof.

And what we call our own personal Christ-nature comes to its full manifestation, and it is accordingly giving forth of its very best, not because it wills so to do, but simply because it cannot otherwise.

Therefore it is that in this most holy communion of the several Christ-natures of those who are not in this body as of those of us who are yet in the physical, the blessedness of the giver of blessedness is the blessedness of all, and the health of the giver of health and the beauty of the giver of beauty is actually present in thy innermost consciousness, my companion worker, there in staying power ever to abide; for it goes never utterly away, but ever increases to the fulness of the Christ-beauty in thy whole nature.

A very homely yet true and beautiful illustration of this I have often used, and it is that, even as in the cooking together in one vessel of various vegetables, the virtues and flavours of all are brought forth more intensely than if cooked separately, inasmuch as the virtue of the one draws forth the virtue of the other, so it is in this most holy fellowship of the unseen and the seen in the service of Healing, as in all social service.

For we are only at our best when we are serving with, for, in, and through one another.

✠ ✠ ✠

And now, as the beautiful and natural outcome of this most heavenly communion in the very body of the Lord of Life, we rise to give thanks for the great joy and privilege of service, and for the most sweet and vital food we have indeed received as the personal blessing that never fails to come with this most holy service of healing.

And in this spontaneous offering of the love of the grateful soul is the true and original, live and eternal, human and divine eucharistic oblation of the whole heart-love unto the one, ever-present Giver of the Bread and the Wine, even of His own very near, warm and vital presence. And they who do participate in this feast know that indeed it is in the very power of the real Presence. Nor can they now doubt that the Blessed One is indeed their minister or servant in Life.

This thank-offering of our love may be expressed in such words as: We thank Thee, the Giver of all good, for thine own presence with us here. For in thy presence thou hast given us all the good we need for the quickening and nourishing of our spiritual nature. And we vow in thy presence and in the presence of our unseen companions as in the presence of one another, that even as thou hast given us now of thy best so we shall ever give, in thy strength and in thy name, of our best to all these little ones of thy body in this great creation, whose need calls to us for the service of love.

And so in the same way, and duly following in its order, comes the spontaneous forth-sending unto the soul of our people, of all these warring peoples, and to the soul of our world, the peace, the great peace that has come into our midst in the presence of the Lord of Love, the Prince of Peace.

For the peace-consciousness being then actually felt of all, and known to be the very breath of the Healing Christ, can be gifted by every live soul present, in whom it manifests unto the needy ones of our world; and in the power of the One who is now in us as the Spirit of Peace we can say: O Peace, O Great Peace of God, we give thee freely and fully, even thee, the most precious one of our nature, unto this needy soul.

Freely and fully, O Christ-blessedness, hast thou given thyself to us, freely and fully do we yield thee now unto whomsoever may and will receive thee. For thou alone, even thou who art the Love of God, art the healer of all these peoples even as of us all.

And until we all learn of thee, the Servant and Lover of all, the only wisdom of Life, and know that it is better to serve than to be served, to give a good than to take it away, to love than to be loved, we cannot enter into the great peace of the one life. Even so come quickly, O thou who art the wisdom and the peace of God. Amen. Amen. Amen.

Be it always well understood that in this most holy service of healing there is and can be to the healer no differentiation whatsoever between the dead and the living; for, to those who know, there are no dead; and it is simply a common-place fact that to them death is not; for God, who is Life, alone is.

I am, even now, in the service of the comfort of one of Christ's own little lambs, even the gentle soul of the white Lily, who has been both my good mate in the work of my life for over twenty years and the little darling of the care of the Christ-mother in me, and who has just laid aside her robe of flesh.

My pet name for this child of the healing hand has been "Jesu's little lovie," for as they who know her, or have read either "The Brotherhood of Healers" or "The Lady Sheila," know well, her distinguishing beauty and all-winning charm and her truly marvellous power as a healer was in and through this child-nature.

✠ ✠ ✠

Now, for the help of my companions who would serve thus, I shall in few words tell how I am moved to work for the comfort of this little one.

Soon after she had passed, the joy of her angel-band as they bore and welcomed her into her heavenly home, began to sing in me as "The Lord hath taken her," in the very words of her own writing (see "The Unclothing of the Flesh," in "Breathings of the Angels' Love and Stories of Angel Life"), and this song kept singing in me these two days. Thus has she been set free and stayed in the comfort of the Great Love through the service of the singing of this song in me.

And on the third day the little one began to awaken into the consciousness of her new life, but yet as a very little child just awakening out of a long troubled dream, and this word of comfort kept whispering itself in me: It's all well, dearie, it's all well, You are at peace in your own home, and your own Jimmie is with you. And she again passed into the sweet and quiet sleep of recreation.

And thus I was allowed to work with the heavenly companions in mothering the new-born into the greater life; for this period of rest or deep psychic sleep is needful to her vital body because of the weariness of the whole nature through these seven long years of her vicarious suffering.

As a very feeble illustration of this mode of vicarious service I would ask you to read "The Afterword" in "The Crucifixion and Resurrection of the Soul of Germany." Indeed this is the last word that came to me through this holy vessel of the great compassion of our Christ, the Heart of God.

I now give what may be received as a communion address to all those who have participated in this the innermost service of the body of the Lord of Life.

For we know that we have here the very reality, the whole content, essence and substance of the Great and Holy Eucharistic Service of Life.

And we declare that it would not be possible for us who fulfil this most holy ministry in the spiritual or formless degree to return to the use of the needless material form.

And when we see our brethren so returning we can only say that they are for a time, howsoever otherwise by subtle argument it may be made to appear, made subject, because of a certain need of their nature to the law of the mere psychic realm.

For in Christ alone is the great service of Life, and it is in the pefect liberty of the children of the free spirit and subject only to its law.

✠ ✠ ✠

And here now, fellow-ministrants in this most holy service, in and through your human soul your flesh and your blood has been poured forth anew, the life of the Christ of the Ages of our race.

And this is the agelong forthpouring of the life of God. And it is ever flowing through the gift of self in the Great Love service of every human soul.

For Love alone it is that enrobes and empowers, that initiates and renders efficient unto the receiving and using of all the powers pertaining to this most holy service of the body of God.

And you, my sister, have love even as I have love; and she alone who is great in the self-giving love is great in the service thereof.

Sister, brother in the family of the one great Christ of mankind, I ask you, is there anything that is lacking for the satisfying of your whole nature in this most holy service of Life?

Nay, nay, ye find nothing of good awanting, and ye know that ye are in the whole work of the self-giving Lover of man, ay, you my sister, as truly in every respect as I your brother.

And ye know that no power or faculty of the service of the body of God symbolized in the external rite of the great communion is not here, and that here, even here in this service, you are ministers and participants in the very essentials of its being.

Ye know that here ye serve in the very vitals of Christ.

For ye are in the whole wisdom of the self-giving Love, and to serve here is to serve in the live Blood of the Body of the Lord of Life.

And once ye have known that it is so, once ye have really tasted of this holy thing, ye could not, no, not even for Love's own sake, ye could not return to the old-time form, ye could not, once having truly known the liberty wherewith the Christ of your nature has made you free, rebind yourselves by the use of incantation, or rite, or ceremony, or form.

The one holy Eucharist of man and beast.

I have now and then, for the sake of the little children who love and are helped by a simple rite, at the close of our spiritual feast, partaken with them of the communal bread and water thus as at Bingley yestre'en.

I had been teaching these Yorkshire women how to bake pure unleavened bread by simply mixing flour—whole-wheat being chosen of course—and water, kneading it well without salt or any raising or lightening ingredient, and laying it on the hearth tiles under the kitchen or sitting-room fire until slowly baked. This is, as you will see, the true, the simple, the classic mode of baking good bread.

One of these loaves I broke into small pieces, and saying to them:—"This is the live body of God broken for your food, for in it the God-life is brought into your present degree of existence, and it is God in this bread that nourishes you, and without the God or Life principle in it it would not nourish your body," handed it round to these people, so that they might taste and prove that sweetness, which indeed they did, and by which experience to me were converted there and then to the true way of baking bread.

And when we had eaten the bread, I passed round the cup of water saying:—"This water is the fluid-body of God, for in it is the life of God given to you for your cleansing and your refreshing. Drink ye all of the cup of God's life."

And thus a very simple and holy rite was fulfilled for the comfort of these little children of the Christ-body and they went away well satisfied, for they had learned a very useful lesson and understood the meaning of it all.

✠ ✠ ✠

So many of the virtuous things of life are cast into the waste through our ignorance; and in God the economy of nature is perfect.

During these weeks of my sojourn among the spinners and weavers of Bradford, I've been saving many of them from the torments of this flu-malady by getting them to boil the celery-tops usually thrown away, and drinking the tea. Why, even from the coster's barrow on the London streets have I gathered, during these months of shortage of green foods, abundance of an invaluable vegetable virtue in the tops of the spring onions always torn off and cast into the waste, and many a pocketful of these have I gladly accepted as the gift of these friends.

✠ ✠ ✠

Half-way up Kingston Hill is a favourite resting-place of mine. It is on the protruding branch of an old elm, and affords such a gently yielding lean-to against the trunk that I usually avail myself of its kind invitation to sit down when passing that way.

The other morning, as I sat there listening to the *Eté de St Martin* song of a beautiful black yellow-bill, a U.D. carter drew up his old horse just opposite me. He was of the ordinary, uninteresting, nondescript type of the English yokel, and one would imagine, from appearances, that there was indeed little of either mental or spiritual intelligence in him.

But when he drew out a bunch of hay, and began giving it to his horse, handful by handful, I felt the power of Love arise within me, and I went over to him and said:—"You know, dear fellow, that in one of the old Psalms it says that these beasts ask their meat from God, and God gives it to them. And that means that you are now one of God's own hands, giving his food to your old horse."

And the dull face lightened, and from the expressionless eye darted a glint of true recognition; and that was his only word of response.

But the soul of the dear old brute also spoke the same soundless word, and sure as I now say it, while he slowly ground the hay, I could see and hear him say:— Yes, you are right; and it is even so. God is giving me of his own body for my food, and this is my Eucharistic feast And indeed, indeed, it was so to me.

(Note for page 42.)

But were I to tell you of the number of declarations I've had during the past 25 years from many of the most worthy and sane souls now incarnate, which all go to prove that they and I and this ancient Jesus-band were, and still are, one fellowship, the most critical of my readers would admit that I have at least good reason for seriously considering what it all means, if not of accepting their declaration as a true word of actual fact.

Some Stories for the Children of the New Day.

The Story of the Queue.

This is New Year's Day, 1918, and I've been standing in a queue for a long time on the frozen pavement of Edgeware Road, where, last week, two little children were trampled to death by the crowd of margarine hunters.

A policeman is now managing these poor people so well, and it is all done through the power of his simple kindliness.

My heart became full of blessing as I watched this man radiating unconsciously the warmth of good cheer; and when at last I had got a bit for the women folks at home, I said to him, taking him by the hand:—" I don't fancy, my dear fellow, that you have any idea of the great service you are rendering to these people by your kindly smile and your sympathetic touch. It is God's own smile that shines in your face."

"No, sir," he said, "I never saw it like that. But I thank you and wish you a good new year."

☦ ☦ ☦

It is now my practice never to lose the service of any experience that the good Hand of Life presents to me, and as my experiences in these queues have been so very, very rich in lessons and in the opportunity to serve the present needs of these little children of the Father-Mother Christ, and as I feel that it would interest many of you to be brought into live contact with the spirit of something you have not been allowed to see, I give you these few touches from my hand now.

I do love the poor, and I do feel myself always at my best among the working people, to which class, through this birth, I myself have the honour and privilege to belong.

And so, when I go among them, they feel that I am, in a way, one of them, and I don't think that they hide from me much of their rich humanity!

How sweet to feel their comradeship of need, their fellowship of want, and how readily they receive and respond to any little touch of self-effacement, or the example of putting the chance of the neighbour before your own.

How sweet to know that you are shedding over that mingled crowd of humble souls the power of the Great Lover and the very blessing of the healing Christ.

It is so simply, so easily, so naturally, so unpretentiously done here as everywhere, if only we will it so; the little touch or caress of love on the heads of the children who stand beside you, or the gift to those ever-ready little mouths of a bit of cake, is a sure and easy and natural way of opening wide the whole nature of these people for he receiving of the great blessing of the holy Presence.

And you are in and feel, the joy of this common soul when at last, after an hour or two of waiting, they see the van loaded with this precious margarine coming round the corner.

Their fun then is at its full, and the carman gets his good share of their blessing and their banter.

Indeed, indeed, if you, even as a student of human nature, would taste the bouquet, simple, rich, yet unalloyed of the real cockney genius, and I do not know of anything to equal it of its kind, you could not do better than take your place in a London margarine queue.

The Story of seeing only the good.

I have been called to serve in Brighton once a month during this year, and this month at the time of the Equinox, the gales and tides and billows being at their best, as you may be sure I took full advantage of them. Last Sunday afternoon, when sitting under a seawall enjoying this great beauty of the power of God, small stones began to rain on me, one or two actually hitting my bare head.

I knew at once that it was only the boys' little mischief genius at work, and as usual at its finest, for lack of anything of interest to do on a Sunday afternoon!

So, instead of taking up a stone and shying it at them, with the sure result, my "pay 'em out" friend, of no more quiet for me that afternoon with my joy by the wild waves, I called up to them, "All right, chums, this is great, come and let's have some fun." The little fellows, ragged urchins most of them, looking over at me, and seeing no doubt that this old bloque was not such a bad sort, came to me one by one until I was actually surrounded by a group of boys very, very much alive, and ready for anything I could give them. And I gave them the gospel of love and service there on that shingle, and so truly were these little men won to love that I had great difficulty to get them to go away from me, and when at last I began to gather the bonnie white sea-moss, telling them I wanted it for sick people's food in London, I soon had from their dear hands as much as I could carry to London!

Now these boys learned that we had been happy because we loved one another, and that there is nothing greater we can do than to love. Nor will they ever forget this lesson, for God spoke to them in and through our play this word of life : Little children, if ye would live, love one another.

☩ ☩ ☩

And yesterday, here at Bingley the same Sunday afternoon experience all alone with about forty boys, following this funny old bloque, and not only calling out pretty words, but actually shying stones after me. These little fellows I kindly invited, and they all came and sat down there on the grass, and when I told them they are all God's children and not the devil's, that the only way of life worthy of them is the life of love and service, these little men received the truth, for it was spoken to them in love. And when I told them that these fags were poison to them, and that they would never grow to be big strong men like me if they smoked, one by one these cigarettes were hid, or put out, or thrown away—no small sacrifice this to Love, as you know. But they did it because they knew it was love that was speaking to them.

Yes, dear fellow-in-service, let us only see, only recognise the good, the angel, the Christ, the God in every soul, the holy thing we can and do love, and assuredly we shall call this good, and only this good, forth into fuller and fuller power in this soul, and so save her from her sins and heal her of her infirmities.

And it was the angel, the Saviour, the Lover in these boys who gave me that right hearty cheer as I went away, for this holy one ever says to the servant of love, "Well done, good and faithful servant."

✠ ✠ ✠

Now this is the wisdom of love, and certainly it is as practical in its service of life as any that the world-spirit can offer us, and of this a wee word now to the point.

For, there is a sharpness of edge, there is a subtilty of power, there is a fineness of touch, that cannot be met by the very finest of the sharpness or wit of the realm of greed and of hell.

I used it some years ago, and as the form of service will surely interest you I'll tell you of it now.

Through an absolute trust and utter cessation from all care concerning my financial interests, which had been imposed on me then because of the very sore and trying conditions of my home life, I had been led to leave all these things in the hands of a friend, who, to say clearly, so abused the trust that it seemed as if I might lose all I possessed.

Well, now, I continued to trust this soul. I never allowed a suspicion to dwell in my heart or to deface my love for this soul, for said I, instead of handing this brother into the hands of the criminal authorities I shall save his soul from the power and the love of lucre. And I know that this has surely been done, for he has served me all these years as a brother.

✠ ✠ ✠

I was lately visiting a friend's home. I was without a hat, and this may have been the cause why a great mastiff rushed at me and in a most determined way made for me with teeth showing.

The right or natural thing was to wield my stick and so meet the brutal attack.

But a finer and a stronger way of doing at once came instinctively to me, and I spoke to the true soul of the dog and I said: "Good doggie; good doggie. You are a good doggie."

And the fury of the dog gradually passed and his rage by-and-by yielded even to a gentle fawning on me. Need I say again to you that this is the spiritual method of healing or of meeting any disorder of any kind.

☦ ☦ ☦

And there is our old coster's pony, who drags the cart of vegetables round our street two times a week.

Now Polly made a nice little snap at me when first I would caress her soft nose and ears. "Ah, sir," said the old coster, "don't you go near she. She'll snap you, the dirty brute."

Well, I did go near she, and I spoke to she, and I said to she "You are a dear bonnie girlie. You are a good, kind pony, and you will not bite me again." And she heard my word, and she received its power, and to make my story short, every time I passed that brute she looked for me, and she was always disappointed if I passed without caressing her, and needless to say, she never once tried to snap me.

And Jesus from the ground Suspires.

The power of the sweetness of the Jesus-spirit has been working in me in a very beautiful way of human service during these months, sorer indeed and more trying to this sensitive human nature than I can ever tell, during which period the whole of the virtue of our fragrant Lily has been slowly gathered by the angel-hands into her own heaven of the new life; and as it will certainly interest you, I shall now tell you of this service.

I have made for these days of mid-summer heat my home-parish of some very, very slummy streets near by that literally swarm with children. I have seen squalor and filth, in the East End, but none to surpass what I have seen in these homes of the poor within half-a-mile of St John's Wood!

Among these children I have gone, making them my friends, chumming with them, and apparently entering into all their little ways.

Now it is not the sprigs of heather nor the twigs of lavender nor the few apples that I have given them that has so drawn these dozens of children round me, that soon as they see me there is the rush of self-abandonment towards me, as they sing out, "Uncle Jim, Uncle Jim," that makes them actually struggle to get a hold of my hands or legs or any part of my body, and so cling to me that it is with difficulty I can get them to go home. No, no, no; but it is, yes I know it is the sweetness of this Jesus-spirit, this holy thing of power that has distilled itself out of my very blood of body and soul during these months of the unceasing pain and labour of my nature; that, as I have said elsewhere, is at once perceived by the child-heart and eagerly absorbed. For it is the sweet mother-love in you, dear soul, just as in me that is ever saying in all the lovers throughout all the ages unto all the feeble little ones, whether of mind or of soul or of body: "Suffer the little children to come unto me, for they are of the innermost heaven of God."

Story of the birth of the Christ-child.

A very quaint and most suggestive story was narrated to me yesterday by my aged artist-friend, C. S. of Liverpool.

While executing these truly marvellous psychic pictures of which I have spoken in "Out of the Mouth of Babes," p. 21, a demon-face of most hideous mein came through his brush. It was the expression or soul of an evil entity, whose very existence seemed to consist in the power to torment or tantalise another soul. . . .

✠ ✠ ✠

Now to resume the story of my dear friend. At the next seance when he took up his brush and palette, great was his surprise to see the head of a most beautiful boy enwreathed in roses, take the place of the demon-head. Now the mystic knows what this means; and you will find my interpretation of it in the "Crucifixion and Resurrection of the Soul of Germany," which can be had for a trifle from the printer of this work.

This boy-head I had copied by my friend, and this copy has been hanging all these years in the dormitory of the Vegetarian Home for Children at Kelmscott, Wallasey, Liverpool, where it can be seen.

The German prisoners.

On the evening of Armistice Day I came once more face to face with a company of German prisoners whom I had been accustomed to greet in an open, simple, and kindly way off and on during the past two years; and indeed, indeed, the spirit of the true humanity, pure, sane, and simple, triumphed there and then, for there could be no mistake what the kindly smile of recognition from these somewhat heavy, yet on a whole well-favoured, and certainly well-fed faces meant; and when I sang out in as plain English as I could:—

> It's comin' yet for a' that,
> When man to man the warld o'er
> Shall brithers be an' a' that,

there was the hearty cheer, showing the response prompt and clear to the call to Brotherhood in these human souls. And, shall I dare to say it, in the kindly smile and friendly glance I caught in the eyes of their bayonetted guards, I could even discern the Jesus Lovelight suspiring from the ground of our human nature!

The Balsam Offering.

This morning of early May, when teaching our little ones the name of the balsam poplar—for in this unusually early spring of 1919 it is already in full leaf of golden green, and in the full richness of its moist, almost gummy fragrance, this inspiration came to me, as so many good things have already come, out of the mouths of Babes.

For I then remembered that the poplar is the common tree of the north of France, and I could tell them that this tree was now shedding its sweet aroma over the graves of the thousands of the boys, German as well as Briton, who gave their all for what they thought to be the best. And unquestionably this offering of their best is accepted by Heaven as the best they could do, and is accounted to them as the best; and so we can now give this sure word of comfort to the many broken-hearted left behind them.

And surely in this forthpouring of their young life there is an offering to peace, shed as a precious balm over the sores of our humanity. For no sacrifice is made in vain.

Here ended the First Edition.

The Story of the Little Loaf of Bread.

Yesterday morning I was early *en route* for Beeston, where the wealth of Sister Isabel's garden, whether in apples or flowers, has been at my disposal for years past. It was about five, and as I walked along the silent streets of Nottingham, I was attracted to the sound of voices that seemed to rise from the pavement. Looking around I saw that a window on the pavement was open, and on looking down I could see two bakers busy cutting off the burnt crusts of the new bread and throwing them into a waste basket.

Now, through an error of the clock, I was on the road just about an hour before I need have been, and as I had left my friend's house without any food and the morning air was chilly, I felt that I could enjoy some of these refuse crusts. So, introducing myself with the usual "Good morning," I told them my story and my desire.

"We would gladly give it you, sir," said the one next the window, "but we dare not," and stretching his hand to a shelf, he took down a dainty little loaf of warm, sweet bread and handed it up to me, which I thankfully received as the gift of the Christ of our human compassion, and broke and ate there beside them as I sat on that pavement! Surely, dear children, that bread was to me, and, through sympathy, to them, the very body of the Lord of Life.

The Story of the Poor Woman's Penny.

During the war-hunger for fuel, when on my wild-apple-tree in Epping Forest, in the attempt to break a dead branch that I might take it home for a poor woman's fire, the great branch broke under my feet and I fell about twenty feet to the frozen ground, landing on the root of my spine, and had I not been helped or protected I must either have been killed or maimed for life. But as soon as I felt the branch give way under me, I instinctively called on the Name, and I do know that I was upheld.

But, as it was, I had to lie for some weeks on a bed of pain in a humble home in East London.

Indeed, I must have been a funny sight when at last I was able to limp out of the house with two sticks, for I had not shaved all these weeks! So no wonder that a poor woman, taking me for a beggar-man, after some hesitation came up and offered me a penny. And I took it from her and said: "I thank you, dear kind heart, and I accept it from you as from Christ; and will you just give it to some one who is in need of it." And the woman understood it well when I blessed that coin and gave it back to her.

But not always have I given back the coins. Thus last Sunday eve I was sitting on a bank by the roadside awaiting some friends.

We were *en route* for a meeting of the Healing Fellowship at Nottingham, and I had a huge bundle of flowers with me for the friends who come to meet us. While sitting there a group of children passed me. They had been searching for flowers through the woods but with little success, for they had only a very few in their hands.

Naturally I did not let them pass without giving them some flowers. After they had passed I overheard a girl, who seemed to be the little mother of the group, say rather sharply: "You should pay for your flowers." And so, after some hesitation, a little boy came back to me and gave me a halfpenny. "Thank you, dear," I said, "I don't sell these flowers, for they are God's flowers, but I'll take the halfpenny and give it to a poor little child from you." Then a wee lassie who had overheard what I said gave me another halfpenny, and then a little boy.

And now, when they were all around me, and I had given them all some more flowers, I told them that in giving these halfpennies to these poor children they were giving them to God. And they quite understood what I meant.

The Story of the Watcher who sang his Songs in the Night.

It was one of these sweet mornings in early spring when the opening dawn seems to breathe forth the one Life. I knew it was time to get up, but though it was yet almost dark, I could hear the first note of the lark far up in the clouds.

So I got up and was soon off to meet the opening day. My walk took me past a roadway where some work was being done, and where I could see in the light of a brazier the face of a man. It was a very striking sight, one well worthy the genius of a Tenier or a Rembrandt, this face of a man lit up by the lurid glow. Nothing but the face was to be seen, for the man was sitting in his box, and so strange was the sight that I stood for a time just to take it in. But by and by he began to sing, and I waited to hear him. He sang several hymns, old fashioned indeed, but all the same, hymns of a true comfort to him. And he sang them so sweetly, and to no ear but the ear of God.

After he had ceased I went up to him, and saluting him, told him how much I had enjoyed his singing. The dear fellow seemed a bit non-plussed at first, but soon he became quite communicative, and he sang some more to me; and ere I went away we were singing hymns together, and even had as our companion in song a young policeman! And never, I trow, did a policeman more enjoy an hour off duty than did that youth as we sang and talked together. For he was on his way back to town, and as we walked homewards he would tell me all the story of his life, just as any boy loves to do.

Now, dear children, this is the story of the nightwatcher who could pass the long hours singing his hymns. But how few of these men can so cheer the weary hours! And I often speak to them, for do you not think that 10 or 12, or even 14 hours, as I understand their weary watch sometimes lasts, is far, far too much to ask any human soul to pass in such lonely, and sometimes very trying conditions? Indeed, I have truly sympathised with them when I have found them asleep!

The Ascension and Assumption of Margaret Leith Bain.

This dawn of Day I saw once more the Light,
the holy Light I've erstwhile seen and felt,
yet was it holier, finer, sweeter far
and more intense than any light I've seen.

And in the rosy centre of the Light
as in a gently pulsing ambient glow
of living radiance purer than the soul
of earth's own sun, I saw the well-known form
of her who gave this body as the best,
the sweetest gift her woman's love could give
unto this man to use throughout this day,
—set in the midst of this deep rosy flame
of ambient glow.

And oh, it shed through presence, upward gaze
of far-rapt blessedness ineffable,
the joy of God, the beauty of the Child,
the ageless beauty of the Holy One,
whom here we name the Christ, but now with her,
merged in its blessedness, for whom we find
no name of earth-born sound.

And, from her robes of azure and of white,
purer than driven snow and deeper far
than the blue sea of our celestial night
or noontide sky,
there breathed a fragrance I could see and feel
and taste and hear as of the soundless word
of her who has become the soul of God,
and uttereth eternally the Word.

And in its voice I heard as of a sound
I ne'er before had heard even with the ear
of the extatic light,
a sound that soundeth far within the deep
unfathomable, the abyss of God,
in Whom the endless ages of this soul
of whitest radiance.

And in that fragrance was the vital word,
the live ambrosia, the holy food
for this sore-wearied man's own angel-soul.

And as it shed itself around, within
and o'er her path, quintessence of her soul,
a life more vital, keener in its joy
and more intense in its essential power,
warmed through my inward penetralia,
and through my heart and soul and mind and brain
and marrow of my bones and of my flesh.

And it became to me the Light of God
and power of vision, power of brain and will
and power to do, such as I've never known,
and she herself the Gift of Life to me.

O Living Light of my own mother's joy,
O vital radiance of the energy
of the one Love's pure flame,
I drink thee, breathe thee now.

O blessed be thy name, and blessed be
the path of thy soul's course, my mother dear
throughout the unborn ages of thy joy.

And blessed be the name of him the friend,
the husband of thy home 'mid Scotland's hills,
the faithful comrade of thy labours here,
the gentle lover of thy new-born life,
the chaste companion of thy new-found joy.

(The gentle mother to whom I inscribe this edition, passed out of this body in August 1919, aged 86.)

I AM OMEGA.

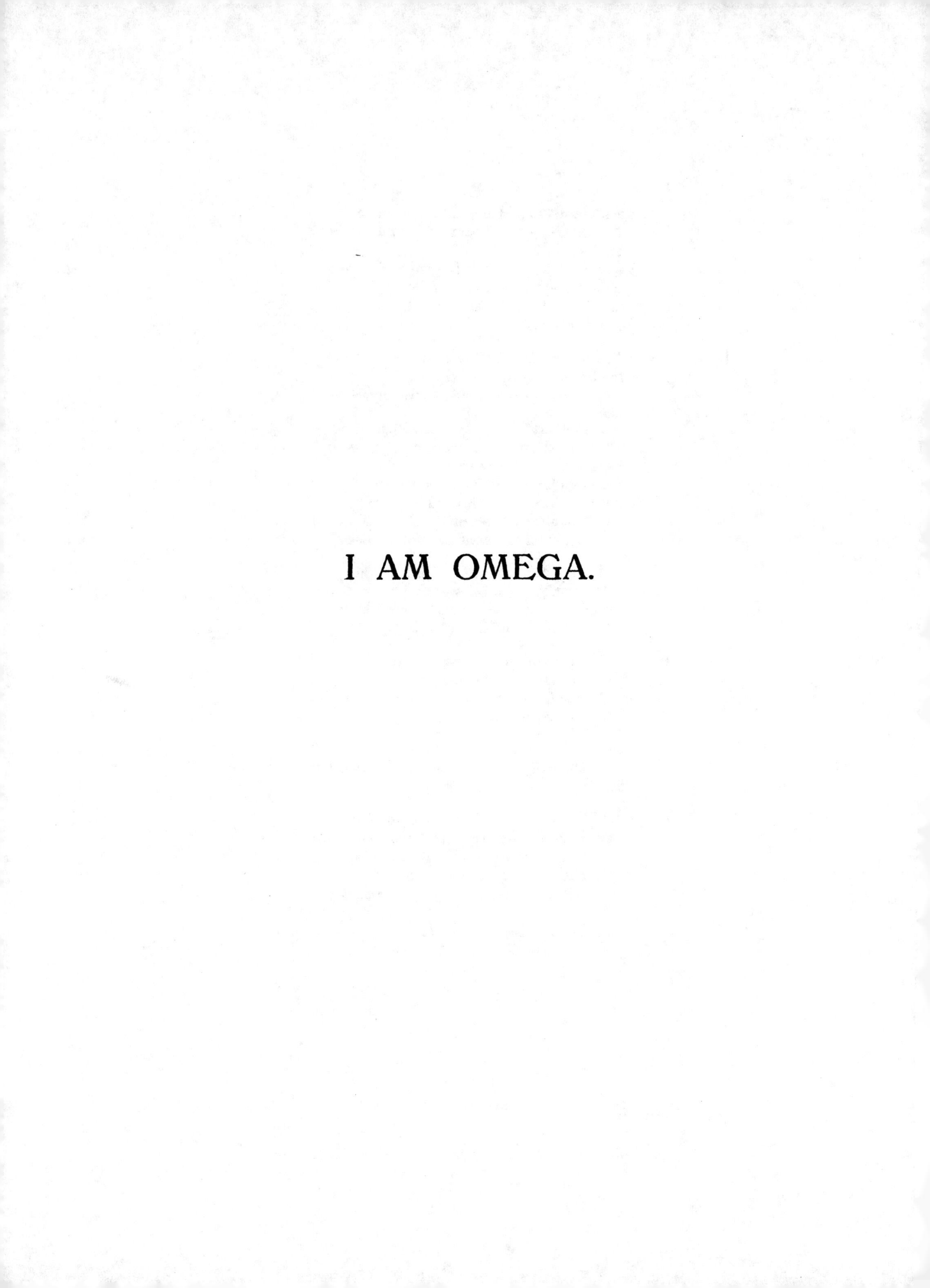